Vatican Museums

EDIZIONI MUSEI VATICANI

GIUNTI sillabe

ISBN 978-88-8271-087-3

Editorial Direction
Direzione dei Musei

Editorial Office
Ufficio Pubblicazioni Musei Vaticani

Photographs:
© Servizio Fotografico Musei Vaticani

Courtesy of Mrs. Edvige Scorzelli: p. 94

© Giacomo Manzù, by SIAE 2011: p. 95
© Filippo de Pisis, by SIAE 2011: p. 97
© Georges Rouault, by SIAE 2011: p. 98
© Marino Marini, by SIAE 2011: p. 99
© The Estate of Francis Bacon, by SIAE 2011: p. 100
© Succession H. Matisse, by SIAE 2011: p. 102
© Salvador Dalí, Gala Salvador Dalí Foundation, by SIAE 2011: p. 103

Courtesy of the Fabbrica
di San Pietro in Vaticano: pp. 170-183

First edition: November 2011

Printed by the Tipografia Vaticana

Reprint	Year
7 6 5 4 3 2	2016 2015 2014 2013

Texts by
Marco Bussagli
(pp. 10-15, 26-31, 76-93, 104-125, 166-183)
Guido Cornini
(pp. 126-127)
Enrica Crispino
(pp. 36-37, 66-69, 72-75, 94-103, 164-165)
Gloria Fossi
(pp. 38-51, 70-71, 128-145, 158-163)
Claudio Pescio
(pp. 16-25, 32-35, 52-65, 146-157)

A publication by:
Giunti Editore S.p.A.
Via Bolognese 165 - 50139 Florence - Italy
Via Borgogna 5 - 20122 Milan - Italy
www.giunti.it

s i l l a b e s.r.l.
Scali d'Azeglio 22 - 57123 Livorno - Italy
www.sillabe.it - info@sillabe.it

Editorial Management
Claudio Pescio,
Maddalena Paola Winspeare

Editor
Augusta Tosone

Translation
Catherine Frost

Graphic design and cover
Lorenzo Pacini

Pagination
Grafica Punto Print srl, Rome

Contents

Colour Code

The colours appearing in the general plan and at the beginning of each chapter in the *Guide* classify the sections of the museum and its works of art according to epoch and style, indicated by different colours:

- Near Eastern Antiquities
  (Egypt and Assyria)
- Classical Antiquities
  (Graeco-Roman Art)
- Etruscan Italic Antiquities
  (Pre-Roman Italy)
- Early Christian and Medieval Art
  (3rd-14th century)
- From the Renaissance to the 19th century
  (15th-19th century)
- Ethnology and History
- Contemporary Art
  (20th century)

Michelangelo, *Creation of Adam*, 1508-1511, detail, Sistine Chapel, Ceiling.

The Vatican Museums are spoken of in the plural because they represent all forms of art, all aspects of human civilisation, at every epoch and every latitude. There is Graeco-Roman statuary overflowing through galleries, halls, and courtyards whose names are famous (The Pio-Clementine Museum, the Braccio Nuovo, the Octagonal Court, the Gallery of Statues, and so on). There are testimonials to the Mediterranean's most ancient civilizations (The Gregorian Egyptian and the Etruscan Museums), as well as the paintings of Giotto and Caravaggio, Raphael, Giovanni Bellini, Leonardo, and Poussin displayed in the Pinacoteca; and the works of Matisse, Van Gogh, Bacon, and Fontana in the Collection of Contemporary Art.

In the so-called 'minor' arts (gilt-glass, ivory carvings, bronze statuettes, mosaics, enamel-work and fabrics) are some of the world's most precious objects, coming from collections previously housed in the Vatican Library and the Tapestry Gallery. In the Pio-Christian Museum, sarcophagi and sculptures narrate the birth, from the fertile trunk of Hellenistic-Roman figurative culture, of an art new in content, ideology, and iconography; while the vast collection known as the Missionary Ethnological Museum displays artefacts from non-European cultures, ranging from Sub-Saharan Africa to China, from North America to Australia.

And there are, of course, the great cycles of frescoes that have given the world the very image of the Bible coupled with the glory of the Italian Renaissance and the Church of Rome: Raphael in the *Stanze*, Michelangelo in the Sistine Chapel.

Today the Vatican Museums are visited by some four and a half million persons each year, coming from all countries, all cultures, all religions, and speaking all languages. At their service is a staff of over six hundred: for the most

Michelangelo, *Delphic Sibyl*, 1508-1511, Sistine Chapel.

part custodians, security and reception personnel, but also administrators, restorers expert in the different sectors, specialists in the various fields, and hence classical archaeologists, art historians, Egyptologists, Etruscologists, epigraphists, ethnographers, chemists in the Scientific Research Laboratory, librarians, archivists, and designers of educational projects.

The volume introduced by these few lines is designed to give visitors a clearer understanding of the wide-ranging, multi-faceted, many-layered and yet universal character of the Holy See's cultural heritage.

A voyage through the Vatican Museums is not an easy undertaking. It can intimidate and disconcert. Passing from Michelangelo to Assyrian reliefs and Egyptian mummies, from the *Laocoön* to Fra Angelico, from Etruscan urns to the artefacts of Australian aboriginals, from the frescoes and tapestries of Raphael to the glassware and ivory carvings of Late Antiquity, from Byzantine icons to the masterpieces of Matisse and Bacon, is an arduous endeavour. But such a voyage fully reveals the historic interest, respect and attention of the Church of Rome for Culture, for everything that has come from the hands of Man the Artist, the only figure that can bear comparison with God the Creator.

In this sense (as this volume will surely help to clarify) the Vatican Museums are the true identifying place of the Catholic Church. As such, they represent its history, proclaim its universality, and mark its destiny.

Antonio Paolucci
Director of the Vatican Museums

History, Collections and Architecture

Three events were crucially important to the founding of the Vatican Museums: the placing of the statue of *Apollo* (130-140 A.D.) by Pope Julius II Della Rovere (1503-1513) in the inner garden of the Palazzetto del Belvedere, whose name it then took; the discovery of the famous *Laocoon* group (40-30 B.C.) on the Esquiline Hill in Rome on January 14, 1506, and its subsequent acquisition for the papal collections; and the purchase of the *Torso* (1st century B.C.) in 1530. This statue, known in the 15th century and studied by both Michelangelo and the erudite archaeologist Ciriaco d'Ancona, was bought by Pope Clement VII de' Medici (1523-1534), who had it placed in the Belvedere Court, where it became known as the *Belvedere Torso*.
These three milestone events reveal the popes' sensitivity to classical art and culture, taking on the value of propaganda by underscoring the relations of continuity between the papacy and Roman ecumenism, whose roots lay in pagan tradition, of which the Church felt itself the rightful heir. Hence the first core of what was to become the world's largest and most important collection of antiquities was installed in the Belvedere Courtyard. To these masterpieces were added others, such as *The Nile*, *The Tiber*, the *Sleeping Ariadne*, and the *Venus felix*, forming the ensemble now displayed in the niches of the splendid 'Court of Statues', known today as the Octagonal Court.
However, no decision to found a real museum, with the systematic collection of sculptures, paintings and documents going far beyond the vogue for acquiring works of art widespread among the nobility, had yet been

View of the Vatican Pinacoteca.

Entrance hall to the Vatican Museums,
with the statue of Giuliano Vangi, *Crossing the Threshold* (1999).

Giuseppe Momo, *Winding staircase,* 1932,
viewed from inside and from below (opposite page).

made. Such an intention began to emerge only during the pontificate of Clement XI Albani (1700-1721), who decided to collect ancient inscriptions, both pagan and Christian, and to found a Museum of Christian Antiquities. The tendency to consider artistic and historical documents as beneficial to society, as precious memorials to be preserved and shared, was, moreover, central to the papal cultural policy. It should always be remembered, in fact, that Clement XII Corsini (1730-1740) first opened the collections of the Capi-

toline Palaces to the public, thereby establishing the modern concept of Museum.
The cultural policy of the Papal State continued to follow this direction under Clement XIV Ganganelli (1769-1774) and Pius VI Braschi (1775-1799), who were the first to plan new buildings specially designed to house the individual collections. To these popes, in fact, we owe the museum named for them: the Pio-Clementine Museum. This policy was fully endorsed by Pope Pius VII Chiaramonti (1800-1823), who added the Chiaramonti Museum and the Braccio Nuovo, while significantly

Spiral rump, 2000.

incrementing the collection of epigraphs. Obviously, the decision to found a museum for the Vatican implied the need for a curator able to fulfil two basic objectives: preserving the collections and incrementing them. The position now held by Antonio Paolucci was occupied in the past by such eminent personages as Antonio Canova (1757-1822), as well as by scholars of international standing such as Deoclecio Redig de Campos (1905-1989) and Carlo Pietrangeli (1913-1995). But this is not the only aspect of the complex

View of the original entrance to the Vatican Museums.

management of the Vatican Museums' vast and priceless collections. The premises that were once the residences of popes, starting with the Palace of Pope Nicholas III Orsini (1277-1280) – the first pope to move here from the Lateran Patriarcate – and continuing through the Borgia Apartment and Raphael's Stanze, have progressively been transformed into modern, functional museums.

This process has involved building projects such as the enlargement of the Pio-Clementine Museum under Pope Pius VI and the construction of a new wing called the Braccio Nuovo between 1820 and 1822, designed and built by the Roman architects Raffaele Stern and Pasquale Belli.

It was also decided to utilise the apartments of Pope Gregory XIII Boncompagni (1572-1585) for the Vatican Pinacoteca, which was then moved several times before 1932, when it was definitively transferred to its current premises, designed by the architect Luca Beltrami.

It can thus be said that almost every pope has taken steps to improve the accessibility and conservation of the Vatican Collections. Up to 1932, for example, the Museums were entered from the San Damaso Courtyard, where the stream of visitors interfered with the diplomatic, political and religious activity of the small ecclesiastical State. It was then that Pope Pius XI Ratti (1922-1939) decided to build the new entrance from the Italian territory, with the monumental winding staircase designed by the Piemontese architect Giuseppe Momo (1875-1940) that is still admired by visitors today, although it has now been replaced by the New Ramp, inaugurated by Pope John Paul II Wojtyła (1978-2005) on February 17, 2000, on the occasion of the Jubilee Year. It would certainly be reductive, however, to describe the evolution of the Vatican Museums as no more than a con-

tinuous improvement in accessibility to the existing heritage. On the contrary, that heritage has been constantly incremented over the years. With the development of such new disciplines as ethnology and cultural anthropology, for instance, the Missionary-Ethnological Museum was inaugurated in the Lateran in 1926. It was moved to its new seat at the initiative of Pope John XXIII Roncalli (1958-1963), who commissioned the architects Vincenzo, Fausto and Lucio Passarelli to design the premises. Completed under the pontificate of Pope Paul VI Montini (1963-1978), this museum was opened in 1973.
The Collection of Contemporary Art, established in the same year, was instead a sign of the times, heralding the Church's renewed interest in contemporary developments in art.

Marco Bussagli

Aerial view of the Vatican Museums complex.

Gregorian Egyptian Museum

The Vatican's collection of Egyptian antiquities was inaugurated in 1839 under the pontificate of Pope Gregory XVI Cappellari (1831-1846) who chose Luigi Maria Ungarelli as curator. Many of the objects displayed come from excavations in Rome and its environs, or in Hadrian's Villa near Tivoli, showing how interested the ancient Romans were in Egyptian art. Over the years many other pieces have been donated, purchased from private owners, or brought here from the Church's other collections. The presence of Egyptian art in the Vatican stems on the one hand from the ancient relationship between Rome and Egypt, on the other from the Church's interest in the Pharaonic culture. The ancient civilization of the pharaohs developed in North Africa, along the course of the Nile, starting three to four thousand years before Christ and continuing up to Roman times (1st century B.C.). Its cultural periods are traditionally classified as: Pre-dynastic Period; proto-Dynastic Period; Dynastic Period, divided into Ancient, Middle and New Kingdom; Late Period and Ptolemaic Age.

In the art of Ancient Egypt, representations of the human figure are schematic and highly idealized. Artistic expression is linked mainly to religion, to the cult of the dead and to veneration of authority, both earthly and celestial. Figurative conventions make Egyptian art clearly recognizable: figures shown in profile but with the bust, shoulders and eye viewed frontally, one leg advanced a step ahead of the other.

Room III. Replica of the Canopus in Hadrian's Villa, near Tivoli (Province of Rome).

Ramses II Enthroned
XIX dynasty, 1279-1213 B.C.
from Heliopolis
black granite; 120 x 65 x 55 cm
inv. 22673
Room I

The 'Lady of the Vatican'
3rd century A.D.
from Antinoe
linen; 200 cm long
inv. 17953
Room II

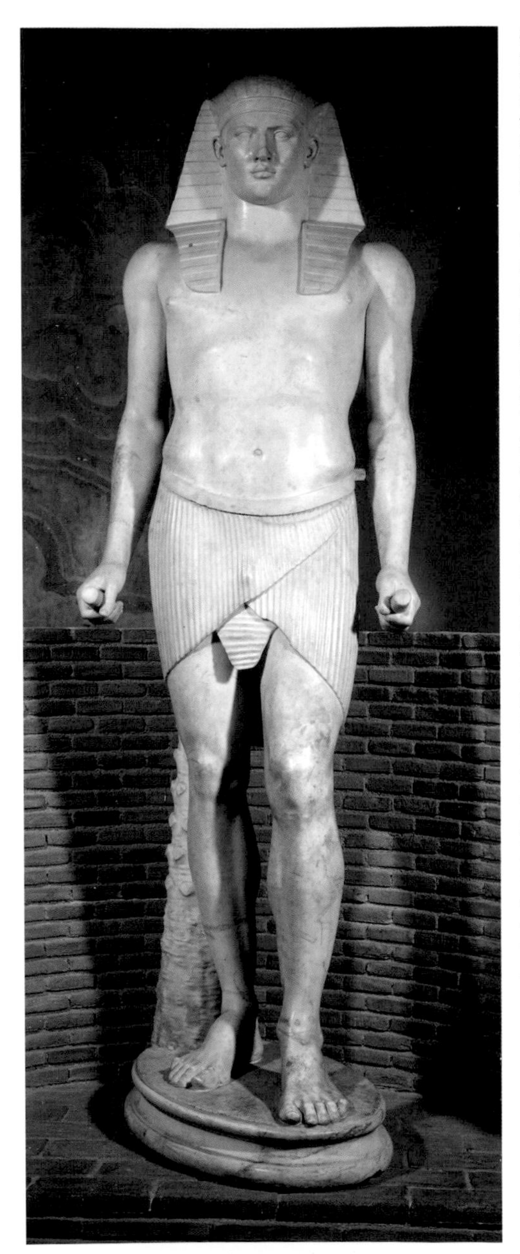

Osiris-Antinous
130-135 A.D.
from the Pecile
of Hadrian's Villa
white marble
h. 241 cm
inv. 22795
Room III

The third room in the museum is dominated by the replica of the most evocative part of the villa built by Emperor Hadrian in 117-138 A.D. at Este, near Tivoli, a short distance from Rome. The Canopus in Hadrian's Villa is named for the one on a branch of the Nile. With statues, basins and architectural elements, it reconstructs an idealized Egypt, which originally included not only a Canopus but also a Serapeum, or temple of Serapis. This sculpture portrays Hadrian's favourite, Antinuous, in the guise of the Egyptian god Osiris. Antinuous died by drowning in the Nile, in Middle Egypt, where the city of Antinoe stands today, founded in his honour by the emperor. In Egyptian thought, anyone who drowned in the Nile, as the god Osiris had done, was identified with him, even in the afterlife.

Anubis-Hermes

1st-2nd century A.D.
from Anzio
parian marble
h. 155 cm
inv. 22840
Room IV

This is a Roman re-interpretation of the Egyptian god who watched over the mummification process and accompanied the deceased to the Other World. It comes from Villa Pamphilj at Anzio, on the coast not far from Rome.

Torso of a Baboon (or Thot Cynocephalus), called Cacco

159 A.D.
from Rome, Campus Martius
beige marble
h. 110 cm
inv. 22833
Room IV

This is another Roman interpretation of Egyptian art, made by Greek artists working in Rome. It is the God Thot, represented as a crouching baboon. By the people of Rome, the name 'macaco', was then distorted into 'Cacco', giving rise to the name of the church called Santo Stefano 'del Cacco'.

Colossal statues of *Ptolemy Philadelphus II* and *Arsinoes II*
Ptolemaic Age,
285-246 B.C.
provenance uncertain
pink granite
h. 276 and 270 cm
inv. 22682 and 22681
Room V

The statues of *Ptolemy Philadelphus II* and its companion piece portraying his wife *Arsinoes II* belong to the Graeco-Roman period of Egyptian art. Their provenance is uncertain. The two sculptures were probably brought to Rome and placed in the Horti Sallustiani by Emperor Caligula in 37-41 A.D. Caligula, was in fact fascinated by Egyptian culture and its cult of royal divinity.

Torso of King Nektanebos
380-362 B.C.
from Nepi (northern Lazio)
black granite
h. 80 cm
inv. 22671
Room V

Winged Genius kneeling in adoration of the Tree of Life
883-859 B.C.
from the North-West Palace of Nimrod
breccia
h. 77.5 cm
inv. 14989
Room IX

Room IX of the Egyptian Museum displays works coming from Assyria (the northern part of today's Iraq). This relief carving, from the Neo-Assyrian period, decorated one of the monumental buildings constructed on the acropolis of the city of Nimrod by King Ashurnasirpal.

Chiaramonti Museum

Charles Maurice de Talleyrand-Périgord (1754-1838), better known merely as Talleyrand, mastermind of the Restoration and the new map of Europe after the Congress of Vienna (1814-1815), designed to keep French territory intact after Napoleon's defeat, scornfully referred to Antonio Canova (1757-1822) as 'Monsieur l'Emballeur', *that is, 'Mr. Packer'. The great artist from Veneto was, in fact, living in Paris in 1815. As General Inspector of the Antiquities and Arts of the Papal State, a position assigned him by Pope Pius VII Chiaramonti in 1802, Canova worked diligently to retrieve the works of art taken to France by Napoleon, who had planned to make the Louvre one of the world's greatest museums, named for him. It was only the French defeat at Waterloo that kept this plan from becoming reality. In the early 19th century the pope founded the Museum that took his name, as a place for displaying great Graeco-Roman sculptures. The long gallery was set up by Canova himself, and still today the arrangement of the statues closely follows his original project. This occasion was taken to celebrate the glories of Pius VII's pontificate and his active, unflagging interest in Italian culture and art. Pope Chiaramonti was, in fact, the first to promulgate a law on the artistic heritage (1820), conferring on works of art the status of public property. For this reason, the lunettes adorning the 300 meters of exhibition hall – divided into 30 bays per side – recall the salient moments in the pope's tireless activity. Outstanding among the lunettes, painted by artists from the Accademia di San Luca between 1803 and 1817, is the one in bay XLI painted*

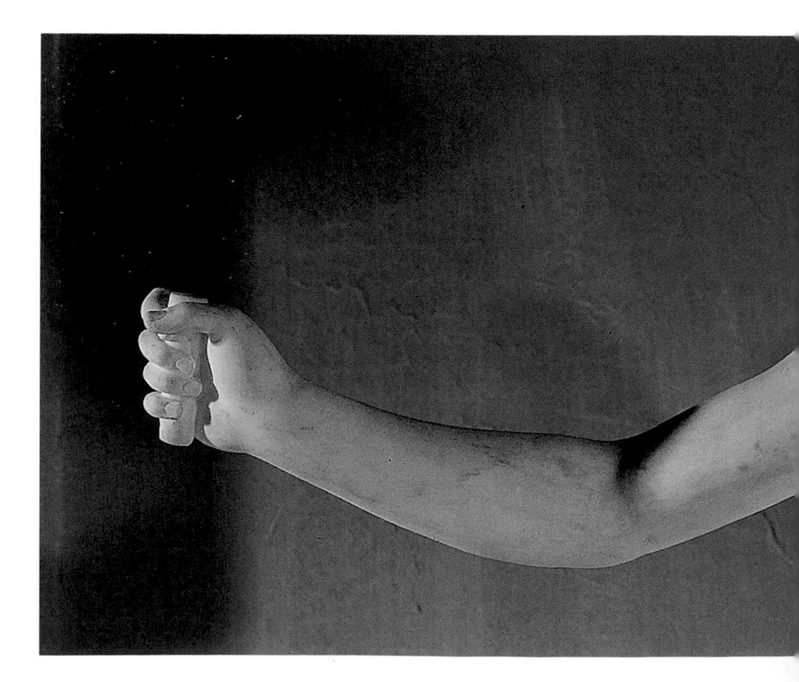

by Luigi Agricola (c. 1750-1821) commemorating the Museum Claramontanum Pioclementino adiectum. *It is an allegory (with the winged figure of* Aion, *Eternity) of the founding of the Chiaramonti Museum* adiectum, *that is, 'adjacent' to the Pio-Clementine Museum. The lunette celebrating the return of the masterpieces to the Vatican collection is instead by the great Francesco Hayez (1791-1882). The marble bust of Antonio Canova, paying due homage to the famous sculptor's tenacious efforts and love of Italy, reminds us that he had worked on Pope Chiaramonti's collection since 1807, the year the Museum was founded, dividing the exhibits into 60 bays indicated by Roman numerals. Over a thousand statues are collected here, mostly Roman copies of lost Greek originals, like the group of* Hercules and his son Telephus *(inv. 1314) in bay IX, where the first statue derives from a Greek work dated to the 4th century B.C., the second from an original of the Pergamon school, 3rd century B.C. An equally notable work (bay XXI) is the* Eros Stringing his Bow *(inv. 1509), a marble replica of the famous bronze by Lysippus.*

Eros Stringing his Bow, detail, 1st century A.D., h. 125 cm, inv. 1509.

Ganymede with Eagle

2nd century A.D.
marble
h. 140 cm
inv. 1376

The sculptural group of *Ganymede with Eagle* was inspired by the verses in the *Metamorphoses* of Ovid (Publius Ovidius Naso, 43 B.C.-18 A.D.) describing the loves of Zeus (X, 151-158), with the abduction of the youth whose beauty had enthralled the father of the gods. Zeus, transformed into an eagle, flew with the boy to Mount Olympus, where he made him cupbearer to the gods; hence Ganymede is depicted in the sculpture holding a cup. The group in the Chiaramonti Museum was found in 1780 along Via Tuscolana, in the Quadraro district, by Giovanni Volpato (1735-1803) and restored by Bartolomeo Cavaceppi (1717-1799). It is a marble from the 2nd century A.D., the copy of a Greek original bronze from the 4th century B.C. Note how the youth, wearing a Phrygian cap that recalls his Asian origins (he was in fact a shepherd from Troas), exchanges a glance of complicity with the eagle, which is in reality the god Zeus.

Portrait of Cicero?

Age of Trajan
marble
h. 74 cm
inv. 1359

This is probably an early 2nd century A.D. copy of a personage famous in the late Republican era, long throught to be a portrait of Marcus Tullius Cicero (106-43 B.C.), the great Roman lawyer, jurist and statesmen whose writings and oratory reached the highest peaks of Latin literature, leaving on it an indelible trace.

Head of Augustus

Age of Claudius
marble
h. 59.5 cm
inv. 1639

The Vatican Museums possess several portraits of Octavius Augustus (63 B.C.-14 A.D.), beginning with the famous one found in the vicinity of Prima Porta. This version posthumous, reveals the psychological traits of the first Roman Emperor (1st century B.C.).

Ulysses

1st century A.D.
marble
h. 97.3 cm
inv. 1901

The statuette portrays Ulysses, the Greek hero of the *Odyssey*, one of antiquity's two most famous poems, written by Homer (8th-7th century B.C.).
It is a Roman copy from the 1st century A.D. that formed part of a group with Polyphemus derived from a Greek original dating from the 3rd century B.C.

Lapidary Gallery

'To he who extended the boundaries of the Roman / Empire, Our Lord / Flavius Julius Constans Maximus / victorious the world over and / and ever noble conqueror, / Memmius Vitrasius Orfitus, illustrious Senator / for two terms / prefect of the Urbs, for three terms Judge Imperial Vicar / devoted to the gods and to the majesty of the Emperor'. These are the words that Memmius Vitrasius Orfitus – twice prefect (from 353 to 355 and from 357 to 359) – had engraved on some bases of the statues of Emperor Constans II (337-361) in the Roman Forum, as his personal homage to the sovereign. Although the statues have now vanished, two of the bases are conserved in the Vatican Museums; one of them, intact, in the Cortile della Pigna, the other, fragmentary, in the Lapidary Gallery, (XXXIX, 13; the other two fragments are in the Roman Forum, along with the third twin base, intact). The Gallery occupies the second section of Bramante's wide corridor that bounds the eastern side of the Belvedere Court. The Lapidary Gallery is open to visitors upon request. For those who have the chance to read some of the 3,400 epigraphs conserved here, it is like listening to the voices of men and women 'recorded' in the

*marble. In the Gallery we find, in fact, in addition to the dedication of Memmius Vitrasius Orfitus, testimonials of other official acts such as the one recorded on the pillar of the freedman Adrastus. As custodian of the Column of Emperor Marcus Aurelius (161-180 A.D.), Adrastus was authorised in 193 A.D. to build beside the monument, in place of his original hut (*cannaba*), a finer residence for which he was supplied with* tegulas omnes et impensam, *that is, 'all of the tiles and building materials'. Fragments carved with figures are also displayed, such as the altar of the knife manufacturer Lucius Cornelius Atimetus (1st century A.D.) depicting the shop of this artisan, with all of the knives hanging on the walls. The collection was formed gradually over the course of the 18th century and was arranged by the epigraphist Gaetano Marini (1740-1815), who grouped the pieces according to subject and typology.*

View of the Lapidary Gallery.

Braccio Nuovo

The Braccio Nuovo (new wing) runs along the south side of Cortile della Pigna, separating it from the Cortile della Biblioteca, which is in turn separated from the Cortile del Belvedere by the wing of a building extending parallel to the Braccio. The Roman architect Raffaele Stern (1774-1820), commissioned by Pope Pius VII Chiaramonti, designed the Braccio Nuovo and planned its decoration in 1806. Finished by the architect Pasquale Belli (1752-1833), after the works of art 'deported' by the French troops under Napoleon had been returned to Rome, it was

inaugurated in 1822. A continuation of the Chiaramonti Museum, from which it is entered, the Braccio Nuovo houses important works of Roman art. The long corridor is lined with niches surmounted with reliefs by the Roman Neo-classical sculptor Francesco Massimiliano Laboureur (1767-1831). Opening off the corridor, at its centre, is a great hemicycle.

View of the Braccio Nuovo.

Augustus of Prima Porta
after 14 A.D.
marble
h. 204 cm
inv. 2290

A work symbolic of Roman culture, this sculpture, an idealized portrait of Rome's first emperor, was probably planned around the year 8 A.D. (although the prototype is sometimes dated at 20 B.C.), at the conclusive stage of Augustus's policy of pacification of Rome's vast, strife-ridden provinces. On the cuirass is represented, in fact, the return (in 20 B.C.) of the military insignia lost at Carrhae by Crassus fighting the Parthians (53 B.C.). The marble copy displayed in the Braccio Nuovo was found in 1863 at the villa of Livia, Augustus' wife, at Prima Porta on the Via Flaminia. It was probably sculpted after the emperor's death in 14 A.D. The statue is modelled after Polycletus' *Doryphoros* (a Roman copy of the Greek original bronze, inv. 2309, stands against the opposite wall, facing the statue of *Augustus*), but following the dictates of Roman public statuary, it is not a heroic nude, typical of Greek art. The figure is brought into historical context, instead, by its symbols of power: the *lorica*, a leather cuirass worn by Roman soldiers; and the gesture of the *adlocutio*, used by a general to call his army into battle. At the statue's feet, a cupid seated on a dolphin evokes Venus, legendary progenetrix of the *gens Julia*, to which Augustus belonged. The symbols and personifications adorning the *lorica* allude to the emperor's role and the salient events of his life: the quadriga of the Sun, symbol of power, with the Heavens above and the Earth below; at the centre, a Parthian king returning the Roman insignia, captured in battle, to a Roman general; and two Winged Victories. In the following centuries, the model of the statue wearing a *lorica* was replicated in numerous versions.

Bust with portrait re-worked to represent Julius Caesar
late 1st century B.C.
white Italic marble
h. 58.6 cm
inv. 2309

This bust portrays an older man with a long face and angular features, his skin closely adhering to the shape of his skull. The chin is prominent, the lips thin and tight, the nose – partially integrated in modern times – long and hooked, with deep subnasal fossae. The eyes are deep-set and the broad forehead is scored with wrinkles. The hair falls in long sickle-shaped locks arranged in irregular rows, which become thicker around the temples and over the forehead, where they form a short fringe. The surface of the face shows traces of modern re-working and attempts at 'cleaning' with abrasives. The lower part of the head is not properly finished, and the volumes are roughly carved in abrupt steps. The bust, not original, is a 16th-17th century work that emulates an ancient model. As shown by these technical and stylistic characteristics, this is as an all-round head from a high-relief funerary carving of the Augustan Age, in which the back of the relief has been chiselled out to obtain the volume of the neck and throat. The features of the original personage were then altered to resemble those of Gaius Julius Caesar.

The Nile
1st century A.D.
marble
165 x 310 x 147 cm
inv. 2300

This colossal sculpture is a Roman copy of a probably Hellenistic original. It may have been found in 1513 on the site where a temple of Isis and Serapis stood (in the area now occupied by the Church of Santa Maria sopra Minerva.

The sculpture is an allegory of the River Nile, dispenser with its floods of fertile lands and thus of flourishing crops and prosperity. The main figure is surrounded by sixteen young boys, representing the 16 cubes of height reached by the Nile at flood along with sphinxes, crocodiles and on the base scenes of daily life on the banks of the river.

Cortile della Pigna

The Cortile della Pigna is one of three courtyards (along with those of the Library and the Belvedere) formed of the vast, once undivided sixteenth-century Belvedere Court, of which today's court of the same name is only a part. Designed by Bramante, the ancient Renaissance court, surrounded by buildings, linked the Casino del Belvedere – also known as the Villa or Palazzetto of the Belvedere, or Palazzetto of Innocent VIII Cybo (1482-1492) – to the Sistine Chapel in the Vatican Palace. Of the three courtyards existing today, which once made up the ancient courtyard, the Pigna is the most recent. It was formed in 1822 when the original court, already split in two in the late 16th century by a wing of the Library of Sixtus V Peretti (1585-1590), was divided by the Braccio Nuovo of Pope Pius VII Chiaramonti. The court is named for the huge bronze Pigna*, or pinecone, nearly 4 meters high, from Roman times (1st or 2nd century A.D.) framed by the enormous sixteenth-century niche built by the Neapolitan architect Pirro Ligorio (1513-1583) that closes off the northern end. Standing at the top of a double ramp of stairs, the Pigna bears the signature of a certain P[ublius] Cincius Salvius. Its base is a Roman column capital depicting the* Awarding of the Prize to a Victorious Athlete *(inv. 5119). At the sides are copies of two bronze Peacocks, whose Roman originals are in the Braccio Nuovo. In ancient times the Pigna seems to have been a fountain, spraying water from the tips of its pine needles, in the Baths of Agrippa (inaugurated in 12 B.C.), in the vicinity of the Pantheon. It may instead have been a fountain in the Iseum Campense (more or less between Piazza Sant'Ignazio and the Church of the Minerva), a destroyed Roman temple of Egyptian style and cult situated in the area that was to become the Rione Pigna. This place name would appear linked to the Roman find. However, in the 12th century, before the district acquired this name, the* Pigna *already adorned a basin for ablutions in the atrium of the old St. Peter's Basilica, where it may have stood since the 7th century. From here it was brought to the Vatican courtyard in 1608. At the centre of the courtyard, placed there in 1990, is a modern sculpture by Arnaldo Pomodoro (*Sphere with Sphere*).*

Cortile della Pigna with Arnaldo Pomodoro's *Sphere with Sphere* (1990) at the centre and, in the background, framed by Pirro Ligorio's great niche (1565), the *Pigna* from Roman times (inv. 5118).

Arnaldo Pomodoro
Sphere with Sphere
1990
bronze
diameter 3.30 m
without inv.
Cortile della Pigna

Pio-Clementine Museum

The Pio-Clementine Museum is a collection of classical antiquities – statues, portraits, masks, sarcophagi, mosaics, parts of basins and fountains for gardens – of unique historic and artistic value. The Museum was founded by two popes, Clement XIV Ganganelli and Pius VI Braschi, and is named for them.
It was Clement XIV, in 1771, who first conceived of establishing a museum of ancient art to preserve the wealth of Greek and Roman works of art owned by the Vatican. Many of these pieces had been discovered as early as the 16th century during archaeological excavations in the Papal State. Pope Clement significantly enriched the collections with purchases on the antiquities market, flourishing at the time, and from private collectors.
Pope Clement XIV's museum was housed in the fifteenth-century Palazzetto del Belvedere, built to the project of Antonio del Pollaiolo (c. 1432-1498) under Innocent VIII Cybo (1482-1492). Here, since the time of Pope Julius II Della Rovere, a splendid collection of ancient sculptures widely known and studied in artistic circles had been displayed. To organise the new museum appropriately, Clement XIV commissioned first the architect Alessandro Dori (1702-1772) and then his colleague Michelangelo Simonetti (1724-1781) to remodel the former apartment of Innocent VIII. Hence the inner square – the so-called Cortile delle Statue, adorned with orange trees, where Julius II's ancient statues were placed – became the Octagonal Court, its space enlarged by the addition of a portico. The rest of the building was left unchanged until around 1780, when, at the initiative of Pius VI, several large rooms were set up and the entrance was moved from the papal apartments to the so-called Simonetti Staircase, *on the opposite*

Gallery of Statues.

side. With this new access, a true museum entrance, the premises became a place perfectly suited to public utilisation.
At the death of the architect Simonetti the work continued, and a new monumental entrance was built, the Atrium of the Four Gates (Quattro Cancelli). From here the visitors' route continued up the Simonetti Staircase, *through the Greek Cross Room, the Round Room, the Rooms of the Muses and of the Animals, to end at the Octagonal Court. It had now become a 'modern' museum, designed for harmonic intermingling of the works displayed and the decoration of the rooms, purposely inspired by ancient Roman architecture. Reflecting eighteen-century taste however, the arrangement does not take account of the provenance or chronology of the works.*
Due to practical problems of traffic flow, visitors to the Pio-Clementine Museum now follow the reverse route, starting from Room XII (Square Vestibule), which was the entrance hall of the original Clementine Museum, and ending at Room I (Greek Cross Room), which served as atrium to the museum founded by Pius VI.

Octagonal Court.

Apoxyomenos

1st century A.D.
(Roman copy of a Greek original bronze by Lysippos, 4th century B.C.)
white marble
h. 205 cm
inv. 1185
***Apoxyomenos* Cabinet**

The *Apoxyomenos* Cabinet is named for the statue of an athlete cleaning his arm with a strigil, an implement used by wrestlers and boxers to wipe off sweat and the oil used to keep their adversary from getting a firm grip. The sculpture was found in the Trastevere district of Rome in 1849, during excavation of a building from the Imperial Age. It is a Roman copy of the lost bronze statue sculpted around 320 B.C. by Lysippos. The favourite artist of Alexander the Great, Lysippos was the innovator in Greek sculpture of the transition from the austere classical style to the softer intimism of Hellenism.
Although none of his works have survived, this copy closely matches a description of the original by Pliny the Elder (23-79 A.D.), and is a masterpiece of ancient sculpture.
The figure is caught in a daily act, an almost casual gesture. The arms stretching forward, as well as the slight bending of the body, violate the rules of frontal presentation, and the statue is designed, in fact, to be viewed from any angle.

Apollo Belvedere

130-140 A.D.
(Roman copy of a bronze original from the 4th century B.C. attributed to Leochares)
white marble
h. 224 cm; inv. 1015
Octagonal Court,
***Apollo* Belvedere Cabinet**

Discovered in the 15th century near a monastery in the Monti district, this was one of the statues already placed in the sixteenth-century court of Pope Julius II Della Rovere. It is a Roman copy from Hadrian's age of a lost original bronze, probably by the Attic sculptor Leochares. Admired by Michelangelo, the statue was widely copied in the Renaissance, and highly praised by Winckelmann and Goethe in the eighteenth century. Apollo, in his purest and most classic beauty, appears in the guise of an archer. In his missing right hand he presumably held an arrow just removed from the quiver, and in his left a bow, also lost. Winding around the tree trunk is the serpent Python, defeated by the god at Delphi.

Hagesandros, Polydoros and Athanodoros
The *Laocoön*
40-30 B.C.
marble
h. 208 cm
inv. 1059
Octagonal Court,
***Laocoön* Cabinet**

This sculptural group was found in Rome in 1506, in a vineyard on the Esquiline Hill near the *Domus Aurea*, the Golden House of Nero (37-68 A.D.). It portrays Laocoön, the priest of Apollo who tried to save his city in the siege of Troy, as told by Virgil (70-19 B.C.) in the *Aeneid*.

Certain that the Greek enemies had laid a trap, Laocoön warned the Trojans not to bring the wooden horse left on the beach by Ulysses into the city. To keep Troy from being saved by Laocoön's warning, Athena, the patron goddess of the Greeks, sent two gigantic serpents from the sea, who wound

their coils around the hero and his two sons, killing them. This tragic episode is portrayed at the movement when one of the serpents has sunk his fangs into the body of Laocoön's younger son, who collapses screaming with pain. The other sea monster is about to bite the priest on the hip, as he tries to tear its head away from him
His elder son is struggling desperately to escape the writhing coils. The expressions of intense exertion and pain on their faces, and the dramatic, hopeless attempts of the three heroes to free themselves from the mortal grip, are strikingly effective. Their complex poses are typical of the Hellenistic style. This work, all trace of which had been lost until its discovery in 1506, was probably carved in Rome – as stated by the Latin author Pliny the Elder (23-79 A.D.) in his *Natural History* – by Hagesandros, Polydoros and Athanodoros, three sculptors from Rhodes. In Pliny's day the great sculpture, called by him 'superior to any other' of its kind, stood in the palace of Titus, but it probably dates from 40-30 B.C., when the three sculptors moved from Rhodes to Rome. When the *Laocoon* was found in 1506, Pope Julius II Della Rovere had it moved to the Palazzetto del Belvedere, to be displayed in the court of ancient sculptures, where it was restored, greatly admired, and much copied. Michelangelo, one of the first to study the sculpture, drew inspiration from it for many of his nude figures.

The Animals Room

The Animals Room is a veritable "zoo of stone", displaying statues and mosaics depicting a vast range of animal species. This fascinating room was created between 1772 and 1775, under the pontificates of Clement XIV Ganganelli and Pius VI Braschi, both promoters of art and science. Originally it was also known as the 'Room of Rivers', since it contained the ancient statues of *The Tiber* and *The Nile*, taken to Paris and placed in the Louvre in Napoleonic times (only *The Nile* has been returned to Rome).

The animals as we see them today are 18th century works or fragments of ancient sculptures unearthed at the time of these two popes and 'restored' to form exotic or imaginary creatures, in the wake of Enlightenment interest in natural history. The imaginative integrations were created mainly by the 'marble cutter' Francesco Antonio Franzoni (1734-1818), a native of Carrara (and thus expert in marble), who died in Rome after having worked for Pope Pius VI for years.

Outstanding among the works 'restored' by Franzoni, precious testimonials to late seventeenth-century decorative taste but equally important for the history of restoration, are *The lynx*, *The dog attacking a deer*, *The bear fighting a bull*, *The panther sinking its fangs into a goat*, *The phoenix going up in flames*, and *The sea griffin assaulting a dolphin*.

As regards art history, however, the most interesting sculpture is the Roman statue of *Meleager*, which seems to dominate the animals from its niche against the wall, and has nothing to do with Franzoni's restorations.

Meleager

c. 150 A.D.
(Roman copy of a Greek model in bronze by Skopas, 4th century B. C.)
white marble; h. 210 cm
inv. 490
Animals Room

Found in Rome in the 16th century, this statue dating from the Antonine Age is the most complete among numerous copies of the lost original by the famous Greek sculptor Skopas. The myth of Meleager was well known in Rome, having been recalled by the poet Ovid (43 B.C.-*c.* 18 A.D.) in his *Metamorphoses*.
The Greek hero of the hunt is depicted standing, lost in thought, accompanied by his faithful dog. At his left, resting on a pillar, is his prey: the bristly head of the Calydonian boar.

Leopard (or *Jaguar?*)

ancient fragment (?)
integrated in the late 18th century by Francesco Antonio Franzoni
oriental alabaster, with onyx and *giallo antico* intarsia
53 x 63 cm; inv. 383
Animals Room

This may be the 'little tiger of oriental alabaster' bought by Pope Pius VI from Franzoni in 1795. To simulate the coat of the Jaguar, an animal unknown in Roman times, Franzoni set into the fragment, an oriental alabaster statue of a leopard, the soft stone *giallo antico*, which was in turn inlaid with onyx.

150
138
421

Mithras Slaying the Primordial Bull (Mithras Group)
second half
of the 2nd century A.D.
marble
152 x 180 cm
inv. 437
Animals Room

Bull attacked by a Lion
30-20 B.C.
from Hadrian's Villa at Tivoli
mosaic
62 x 52 cm
inv. 421
Animals Room

Apollo Sauroktonos ('The lizard killer')
late 1st-early 2nd century A.D.
(Roman copy of a bronze original by Praxiteles from c. 360-350 B.C.)
marble
h. 167 cm
inv. 750
Gallery of Statues

The sculpture of the young Apollo killing a lizard is displayed, along with others from Roman times, in the Gallery of Statues, once an open loggia on the ground floor of the Palazzetto del Belvedere. Converted into a Gallery in 1771 by the architect Alessandro Dori (1702-1772), it was enlarged and joined to the Animals Room in 1776, which required the demolition of a chapel frescoed by Andrea Mantegna in the 15th century.
Several copies of the lost original *Apollo Sauroktonos* by the Attic sculptor Praxiteles (active between 375 and 330 B.C.) are known, as this subject was highly popular in Rome. The most famous of them, now in the Louvre, was discovered on the Palatine Hill. The beautiful young god Apollo languidly rests his left arm on a tree trunk. In his right hand is a dart, which he cruelly aims at a lizard (*sauròs* in Greek) crawling along the trunk. The rendering of the adolescent's serenely absorbed gaze, following the direction of his hand, is strikingly effective.

Venus of Cnidos

first half of the 2nd century A.D.
(Roman copy of a Greek original in marble by Praxiteles, 350 B.C.)
white marble
h. 205 cm
inv. 812
Mask Room

The Mask Room, included in the museum in 1780, was originally a projecting spur of the Palazzetto del Belvedere. It is named for the masks depicted in the mosaics displayed here, found in Hadrian's Villa at Tivoli, near Rome, in 1779.
The most famous piece in this room is, however, the *Venus of Cnidos*, a Roman copy of the original by the great Athenian sculptor Praxiteles. The original sculpture, now lost, was so greatly admired in antiquity that an amazing 150 copies of it have survived. The nude goddess, about to bathe, has rested her gown on the vase beside her.
It is said that Praxiteles designed two statues of Aphrodite, the Greek goddess of Beauty (the Roman Venus): one fully dressed, sent to the island of Kos, and the other nude, the most highly admired, which was placed in the sanctuary at Cnidos and was the model for this copy.

Belvedere Torso

1st century B. C.
(copy of a Greek original in bronze dating from the 2nd century B.C., signed on the rock: 'Apollonius, Athenian, son of Nesto')
white marble; h. 130 cm
inv. 1192
Room of the Muses

The *Belvedere Torso* portrays the Greek hero Ajax as he contemplates suicide, seated on a lion skin draped over a rock. Since 1973, this sculpture has stood at the centre of the octagonal room displaying the statues of *Apollo and the Muses*, found in 1775 at the Roman villa of Cassio near Tivoli, in the vicinity of Rome. The Room of the Muses dates from around 1780, like the frescoes on the ceiling, by Tommaso Conca, reflecting the subjects of the statues displayed here. The famous *Belvedere Torso*, instead, had been known in Rome, first in a fragmented state, since the 15th century. In the 1530s it was moved to the Belvedere Garden (hence its name). It was studied and admired by Renaissance artists, among them Michelangelo, who did not dare to integrate its numerous missing parts, as the pope had requested. Admiration for the statue with its muscular body continued into the 18th century, when Johann J. Winckelmann (1717-1768), theoretician of Neoclassicism, called the *Torso* a 'marvellous oak tree cut down and despoiled of its branches and fronds'.

Round Room

One of the most fascinating halls in the Pio-Clementine Museum, the Round Room, built for the new Museum around 1780, is considered the architectural masterpiece of Michelangelo Simonetti (1724-1781).

The rotunda topped by a dome (approximately 22 meters high with outside diameter of 21.60 meters) was apparently inspired by the famous Roman building known as the Pantheon. The floor is decorated with ancient mosaics depicting battle scenes with centaurs, as well as various marine animals and imaginary creatures.

At the centre of the Round Room stands an enormous monumental basin with circumference of 13 meters carved from a single piece of porphyry, an extremely costly marble. It may come from the *Domus Aurea* (*Nero's Golden House*) in Rome. The walls are lined with colossal statues in marble and bronze, all Roman works, some of them copies of Greek originals.

Sarcophagus of Constance

4th century A.D.
porphyry; h. 225 cm; inv. 237
Greek Cross Room

This imposing sarcophagus in red porphyry was made for Constance, daughter of Emperor Constantine I (*c.* 280-337). It comes from the Mausoleum of Constance in Rome, on the Via Nomentana, which became the Baptistery of Santa Agnese. The longer sides of the sarcophagus are decorated with relief carvings of cupids harvesting grapes amid vine scrolls, while on the shorter sides they are pressing grapes in a vat.

Sarcophagus of St. Helena

4th century A.D.
porphyry; h. 242 cm
inv. 238
Greek Cross Room

Like the *Sarcophaqus of Constance*, that of *St. Helena*, the grandmother of Constance and mother of Constantine, comes in all probability from a workshop in Alexandria, Egypt, whose craftsmen specialised in the laborious working of porphyry. The sarcophagus was in the Mausoleum of St. Helena in Rome. In 1154 it was moved to San Giovanni in Laterano to be used as the tomb of Anastasius IV (1153-1154).

Gregorian Etruscan Museum

The first large-scale, systematic archaeological excavations in Lazio, the territory of ancient Etruria, were conducted in the early 19th century. At this time numerous finds, mainly from the necropolises of Vulci and Cerveteri, entered the Vatican collections. The Etruscan section of the Vatican Museums was inaugurated in 1837 under Pope Gregory XVI Cappellari, for whom the Museum is named. In the 1920s the original nineteenth-century layout was scientifically arranged by the director Bartolomeo Nogara (1868-1954). From the very start, this museum differed from the others already set up in the Vatican, which were all Fine Arts collections. The Etruscan Museum immediately appeared as important ethnic and cultural documentation of a culture and period deemed 'mysterious', but which should rightly be viewed as one of the pre-Roman Italic civilizations. The exhibits range from Iron Age artefacts (small impasto vases, biconical burial urns) to orientalizing materials such as the objects found in the Regolini-Galassi Tomb at Cerveteri, to pottery of Greek provenance (the height of fashion in the homes

of wealthy Etruscans), to bronzes, bucchero ware, sarcophagi, statuary (also in bronze, such as The Mars of Todi*), jewellery, stelae bearing inscriptions, and the numerous finds coming from Rome and the territory of Lazio (grouped together in the Antiquarium Romanum) that bear witness to the passage of Roman civilization. The collection is housed on the first floor of the building bounding the northern side of the Cortile della Pigna (just above the Hemicycle of the Pigna), partially designed by the Neapolitan architect Pirro Ligorio (1513-1583). Today the museum occupies 22 rooms, covering a surface area of nearly 2000 square meters. In November 2010, after five years, Rooms XIX-XX-XXI have been reopened to the public with newly designed arrangement.*

A room in the Gregorian Etruscan Museum.

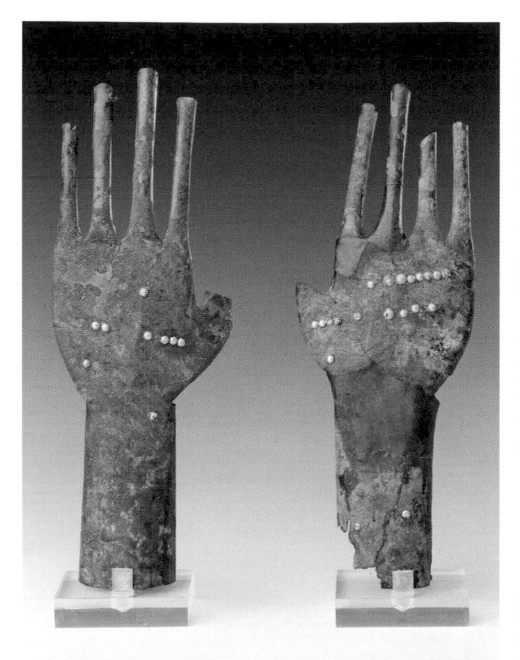

Two hands

early Iron Age,
7th century B.C.
from Vulci
sheet bronze
h. 27.5 and 28.2 cm
inv. 11930, 11931
Room I

These two hands are representative of the earliest attempts in Etruscan art to represent the human figure. In this case, the hands are modelled from a single sheet of bronze slightly bent at the edges and adorned with small gold studs.

Hut-shaped urn

Iron Age, 9th century B.C.
from Castel Gandolfo
impasto pottery; h. 27.5 cm
inv. 15396. **Room I**

Showcase B contains artefacts from the Alban Hills, where Latin civilization had its origins, especially from the excavations at Castel Gandolfo conducted in 1816-1817. The hut-shaped cinerary urns, characteristic of the area and the period (Iron Age, 9th-8th century B.C.), are also found in Etruria. The urn was modelled to resemble the home of the deceased, furnishing crucial information on the houses of the time – simple in shape, with rectangular or oval base, built of reeds, twigs and clay, with a single entrance and a hole at the top to let out smoke from the fireplace.

Chariot
middle of the 7th century B.C.
from Cerveteri
(Regolini-Galassi Tomb)
iron and bronze
inv. 20555
In storage

Room II occupies premises frescoed in 1563 by Federico Barocci (1535?-1612) and by the Zuccari brothers, Federico (1539-1609) and Taddeo (1529-1566), with *Scenes from the Life of Moses and Aaron*. The room is entirely devoted to the materials found in three tombs – the Regolini-Galassi, the Giulimondi and the Calabresi – at Cerveteri, a locality in Lazio on the coast north of Rome. The first of the three tombs, in the Sorbo necropolis, is the most important one in the whole area, and can still be visited on site. Excavated in 1836-1837, it was named after its two discovers (a general, Vincenzo Galassi, and a priest, Alessandro Regolini).
Its lavish grave goods belong to the orientalizing stage of Etruscan culture, a time of flourishing trade with Greece and the Near East. The tomb was built for two occupants of high rank.
The grave goods include a bronze bed, a funerary cart, a chariot (shown here), a bronze throne, tableware in silver and in bucchero, as well as various objects in gold, most notably a great *Fibula* and a breastplate.

Fibula
middle of the 7th century B.C.
from Cerveteri
(Regolini-Galassi Tomb)
gold; 31 x 10 (arc),
23/24 x 3 (cross-piece),
21.7 x 16.4 (disk) cm
inv. 20552. **Room II**

The fibula was a kind of safety pin used by both men and women to fasten clothing. This large, luxurious version belonged to the woman buried in Regolini-Galassi Tomb. It is decorated in geometric patterns as well as plant and animal motifs: lions in the middle and ducklings along the edges. Various techniques were employed in its decoration – embossing, granulation and punching.

Breastplate
middle of the
7th century B.C.
from Cerveteri
(Regolini-Galassi Tomb)
gold leaf and copper
42 x 38.1 cm
inv. 20553
Room II

Like the *Fibula*, this breastplate comes from the grave goods of the woman buried in the Regolini-Galassi Tomb. The embossed decoration on the gold leaf (a one-of-kind piece) consists of concentric bands, each made up of repetitive elements: lions, winged lions, deer and chimeras; at the centre are winged female figures and male figures amid rampant lions.

Bronze Boss
late 6th century B.C.
from Tarquinia
bronze leaf
diameter 40.8 cm
inv. 12461
Room III: Bronzes

This *Boss* is one of eleven, all decorated with the head of lions or of Achelous, a Greek god who personified a river, distinguished by the horns of a bull. A rival of Hercules, he was defeated by the hero after his Twelve Labours. The bosses come from a tomb in the Monte Quaglieri necropolis. Their function is uncertain; they may have served as decoration for a wall or a piece of furniture.

Mirror
c. 470 B.C.
from Vulci
bronze
22.8 x 17.2 cm
inv. 12241
Room III: Bronzes

Bronze mirrors, polished on one side and decorated on the other, were abundant in Etruscan craftsmanship. In this case the mirror is engraved with a scene inspired by the myth of Eos (Aurora), who abducted the young hunter Cephalus.

Cista
late 4th century B.C.
from Vulci
bronze
49 x 28 cm
(without lid)
h. total 38.5 cm
inv. 12259, 12260
Room III: Bronzes

The handle of this cylindrical container is decorated with imaginary figures, the body with an embossed scene of a *Battle between Greeks and Amazons*. It was used to hold toilette articles.

The Mars of Todi
late 5th century B.C.
from Todi
bronze
h. 141 cm
inv. 13886
Room III: Bronzes

The extreme rarity of examples in bronze surviving from the great statuary of Antiquity of Italic sculpture prior to the Roman Age makes this piece priceless. It is a hollow bronze sculpture – made by separately casting and then assembling large parts – portraying a warrior (improperly referred to as Mars). The figure was completed by a helmet (lost), a patera (cup for libations) in the right hand and a lance in the left. These objects, found in fragments beside the statue, are displayed in another showcase in the same room. The sculpture, emulating the style of classic Greek statuary of the time, was found in the Monte Santo locality at Todi, encased in travertine slabs. On the breastplate appears a dedicatory inscription written in the Etruscan alphabet but in the ancient Umbrian language: '*Ahal Trutitis dunum dede*' ('donated by Ahal Trutitis').

Two lions
late 6th century B.C.
from Vulci
nenfro; h. 57 and 58 cm
inv. 14955 and 14956
Room IV:
Stone Monuments

These two sculptures stood guarding the entrance of a chamber tomb, as if to protect a sacred place that should not be profaned by the living

'Bilingual' sepulchral stele
second half of the
2nd century B.C.
from Todi
travertine
61 x 63 x 20 cm
inv. 14958
Room IV: Stone Monuments

Noteworthy among the stone materials collected in Room IV, Stone Monuments, is this tombstone engraved on both sides with a dedication relevant to the construction of the tomb. It is especially interesting insofar as the text is written in two languages, Latin and Celtic, although the latter is written in the North-Etruscan alfabet.

Antefix with head of a woman
c. 500 B.C.
from Cerveteri
terracotta
inv. 13883
Room VI: Terracottas

Rooms V and VI contain terrecottas, both votive and decorative. Coming mainly from ancient Caere (Cerveteri), they belong to the archaic period of Etruscan civilization. In sacred precincts, enclosed by walls and usually consisting of a temple with a forecourt, architectural decoratio ns and objects used in religious rites were found along with great quantities of *ex voto*, most of them representing parts of the body.
These little terracotta figures were brought to the temple as requests for healing the organ represented.
Antefixes such as this one, instead, whose colours are unusually well preserved, served as end pieces and decoration for the tiles under the eaves of the temple roof.

Earrings in the shape of bunches of grapes

middle of the 4th century B.C.
from Vulci
gold leaf; h. max 7.6 cm
inv. 13502, 13503
Room VIII: Gold Jewellery

In 1837, luxurious grave goods were found during excavations in the Camposcala necropolis at Vulci, exemplified by the pieces shown here. In addition to the earrings in the classic shape of bunches of grapes, the grave goods included a laurel-leaf diadem, a necklace with pendants, another oak-leaf diadem and a perfume burner.

Amphora with horse's head

6th century B.C.; from Vulci
Greek black-figure pottery
h. 32.9 cm; inv. 39520
Room IX: The Guglielmi Collection

This room contains objects from the legacy of one of the private collections of Etruscan art, the Guglielmi Collection, donated to the Vatican Museums in 1937. The noble family of the Guglielmi, from Vulci, had formed the collection from excavations conducted on their estates, Camposcala and Sant'Agostino, in the territory of the ancient Lazian city. Until the end of the 19th century the collection was displayed at Palazzo Guglielmi in Civitavecchia. It consists of 800 pieces, mainly bucchero ware, pottery, bronzes and Greek red- and black-figure vases, covering a vast span of time, from the Villanovan age to the Hellenistic period.

The Master of Oenomaus
Urn
early 2nd century B.C.
from Todi
alabaster
40.5 x 81 x 28.7 cm (lid)
43 x 84.5 x 26.5 cm (body)
inv. 13887
Room X: Cinerary Urns

Rooms X and XI contain a great number of cinerary urns from the late period. The Etruscans practiced both interment and cremation of bodies. The ashes of the deceased were deposed in stone or terracotta urns.
The urns in these rooms come mainly from the area around Volterra, Chiusi and Perugia. The materials used reflect the nature of the different territories, with alabaster predominating at Volterra and Chiusi and travertine at Perugia. The urn shown here, probably produced at Volterra, was found at Todi in 1516 and was then reutilized, perhaps as a reliquary. The lid is decorated with the figures of a husband and wife reclining on a 'kline'. The decoration on the body is inspired by the myth of Pelops; specifically, it depicts the moment when Pelops slays King Oenomaus after having won a chariot race (Oenomaus had instituted the race as a challenge to his daughter's suitors who, when defeated, were killed by the king); Pelops managed to win by trickery, causing the death of Oenomaos.

The Dying Adonis
second half of the 3rd century B.C.
from Tuscania
polychrome terracotta
62 x 89 x 40 cm
inv. 14147
Room X: Cinerary Urns

More than an urn, this is a kind of funerary monument, which may have served as crown to a cinerary urn proper. The *Adonis* was found in the excavations conducted by the Campanari family; the father and three sons, all archaeologists from Tuscania, organised the first great Etruscan exhibition, held in London in 1837. It was the event that made Etruscan art known to the public, arousing great interest in the mysterious vanished civilization. With a certain *pathos*, the scene portrays the shepherd Adonis mortally wounded. The young man of rare beauty, contended by Aphrodite and Persephone, died slain by a wild boar – sent by the jealous Ares, or by Apollo – while hunting.

The Troilos Painter
Amphora
early 5th century B.C.
from Cerveteri
Attic red-figure pottery
inv. 16513
Room XIX: Attic Vases
Lower Hemicycle

The Vatican's Vase Collection was started in the 18th century. It was greatly incremented by the excavations conducted in the first decades of the 19th century, which led to the founding of the Gregorian Etruscan Museum in 1837. Greek vases were imported to Etruria on a grand scale for centuries. Owning Greek pottery was a status symbol for the wealthier families, and the trade in vases also led to a local production of similar works.

This vase is decorated with scenes of a procession of musicians and the contest between Heracles and Apollo for possession of the oracle's tripod in Delphi, which the hero – furious because he had not received the oracle from the Pythia – had taken from the temple where it was kept, committing an act of sacrilege.

Exekias
Amphora
540-530 B.C.
from Vulci
Attic black-figure pottery
h. 61.1 cm; inv. 16757
Room XIX: Attic Vases
Lower Hemicycle

One of the most famous works of Greek pottery, this masterpiece was found in a necropolis at Vulci in the early 19th century. In the best-known scene, Ajax and Achilles (whose names appear beside the figures) are throwing dice during a pause in the siege of Troy. Achilles is the winner, since the number written beside him is four, while for Ajax it is three. On the opposite side appears Castor with his horse Kylaros, his brother Pollux and their parents Leda and Tindaros. The amphora is signed by the Attic painter and potter Exekias, whose work is distinguished by minute attention to details.

The Oedipus Painter
Kylix
480-470 B.C.
from Vulci
Attic red-figure pottery
h. 26.4 cm
inv. 16541
Room XIX: Attic Vases
Lower Hemicycle

This *Kylix* – a wide, shallow wine cup with stem, made of pottery – is decorated on the inside with the mythological scene of Oedipus in the guise of a traveller listening to the enigma proposed to him by the Sphinx, a winged monster with the head of a woman and the body of a lion. It lived near Thebes – a Greek city in the region of Boetia, and interrogated travellers with obscure riddles, devouring those who could not answer. Oedipus alone managed to guess the answer, causing the Sphinx to throw itself down a cliff.

The Berlin Painter
Hydria
490 B.C.
Attic red-figure pottery
h. 58.2 cm
inv. 16568
Room XXI:
Sundial Room

Named for the sundial, this room housed a collection of astronomical instruments until 1801. The Berlin Painter, one of the most important Athenian artists of the 5th century B.C., created vases distinguished by a particular glossy sheen.
This *Hydria* (three-handled water vessel) is decorated with a scene of Apollo flying over the sea, seated on the Delphic tripod.

Bell krater
350-340 B.C.
from Paestum
painted pottery
h. 37 cm
inv. 17106
Room XXII:
Italiot Ceramics
Upper Hemicycle

This room displays Italiot red-figure pottery (from southern Italy and Sicily). Italiot pottery was influenced by the Attic tradition. References to the theatre are strong, at times with a less noble and more satirical in spirit. Here Zeus is shown courting Alcmena in the presence of Hermes. From the union of Zeus and Alcmena, Hercules was born.

The Biga Room

This small rotunda topped by a dome, situated above the Atrium of the Four Gates (Quattro Cancelli), is named for the Roman marble group by Francesco Antonio Franzoni (inv. 2368). Illuminated by the beam of light falling from the oculus in the ceiling, this imposing sculpture dominates the centre of the room. Only the body of the chariot and part of a horse date from the 1st century A.D., the rest is the work of Francesco Antonio Franzoni (with the addition of the wheels, the shaft, and the horse on the left) in the late 18th century, when the room it occupies was built by the Roman architect Giuseppe Camporese (1761-1822) for Pope Pius VI Braschi between 1786 and 1794. Along the walls, formed of four niches between pilasters and arched bays, other Roman sculptures copied from Greek originals surround the Biga*: the* Discobolus*, 2nd century A.D. (inv. 2346), coming from Hadrian's Villa at Tivoli, a famous copy in marble of Myron's bronze; and the statue of* Dionysus 'Sardanapalos' *(inv. 2363), as reads the inscription on the hem of the cloak, taken from an original by Praxiteles (4th century B. C.) and dating from the 1st century A.D.*

Biga
1st century A.D.
marble
inv. 2368
Biga Room

Gallery of the Candelabra

The Gallery was originally an open loggia overlooking today's Cortile della Pigna. In the late 18th century, Pope Pius VI Braschi commissioned the architect Michelangelo Simonetti (1724-1781), and at his death Giuseppe Camporese (1761-1822) to enclose the loggia and divide the interior into six sections, marked by arcades supported by columns and pillars. The Gallery is named for the great marble candelabra, some of them dating from the 2nd century A.D., that stand in pairs at the sides of each arcade; they come from the Umbrian locality of Otricoli (Ocriculum). The ceilings were frescoed in the late 19th century by Domenico Torti (1830-1890) and Ludwig Seitz (1844-1908) with scenes from the pontificate of Leo XIII Pecci (1878-1903). The Gallery, nearly 80 metres long, displays various archaeological materials from the Roman Age and numerous sculptures, Roman copies of Greek originals. Outstanding among them are two Roman replicas of Greek originals: Ganymede and Eagle *(inv. 2445) and the* Ephesian Artemis *(inv. 2505), dating from the 2nd century A.D., both found in Section II.*

View of the Gallery of the Candelabra.

Gallery of Tapestries

The tapestries in this collection date from the 16th and 17th centuries. Especially interesting are the Flemish tapestries woven at Brussels between 1524 and 1531 in the shop of Pieter van Aelst, based on drawings by Raphael's pupils, at the time of Pope Clement VII de' Medici. This series is called Scuola Nuova *(New School) or the* Life of Christ *to distinguish it from the* Scuola Vecchia *(Old School) series, consisting of ten tapestries woven by van Aelst (c. 1450-1533) to drawings by Raphael in 1515-1516 (seven of the cartoons have survived, and are now at the Victoria and Albert Museum in London). This series was commissioned by Pope Leo X (1513-1521), who like Clement VII belonged to the Medici family of Florence. Destined to enhance the solemn ceremonies held in the Sistine Chapel where it was displayed for the first time in 1519, the* Scuola Vecchia *series is now in the Vatican Pinacoteca. The* Scuola Nuova *series, hanging on the wall opposite the windows, illustrates the* Life of Christ. *It can be di-*

vided into two groups, each containing six tapestries. The first is dedicated to the Childhood of Christ, the second illustrates episodes occurring after the Crucifixion (of this group, the tapestry depicting Christ in Limbo *has been lost). Among the greatest and most important are the* Adoration of the Magi *(inv 43860) and the* Resurrection *(inv. 43861). In addition to the* Scuola Nuova *series, the Gallery displays other sixteenth-century Flemish tapestries, such as* The Conversion of the Centurion Cornelius *(inv. 43786),* c. 1530, *and* The Death of Julius Caesar *(inv. 43788) from 1549. A series from the following century, woven in Rome between 1663 and 1679 by the Barberini Tapestry Workshop, is instead displayed on the wall with the windows. It illustrates episodes from the* Life of Urban VIII, *whose secular name was Maffeo Barberini, pope from 1623 to 1644 and uncle of Cardinal Francesco Barberini, who founded the Roman workshop in 1627; it was closed in 1683, a few years after his death.*

Flemish Workshop
Resurrection
Brussels, 1524-1531
tapestry; 562 x 954 cm
inv. 43861
Gallery of Tapestries

Gallery of Maps

The Gallery of Maps, 120 meters long and 6 wide, unique of its kind, is found along the route leading to the Sistine Chapel. Of great artistic and scientific importance, it is named for the forty topographical maps frescoed on the walls, forming an immense atlas of sixteenth-century Italy. On the barrel-vaulted ceiling, geography and history are intermingled in religious scenes linked to the regions illustrated below. Built in 1578-1580 by the architect Ottaviano Mascherino (1536-1606), who also designed the adjacent Tower of the Winds, the Gallery had been planned by Pope Gregory XIII Boncompagni. In 1580 the pope commissioned Girolamo Muziano (1532-1592) and Cesare Nebbia (1536-1614) to direct a group of painters and stucco artists, including the Flemish landscape painter Paul Bril (1554-1626) in the work of decorating it, which was completed in three years. On the long walls are thirty-two topographical maps of the Italian regions (each approximately 330 x 425 cm). The maps are accompanied by perspective plans of the major cities and the Papal possessions of the time, which included Avignon in France, along with two maps of Ancient and Contemporary Italy. On the shorter walls are perspective views, in different sizes, of four great Italian ports – Civitavecchia, Ancona, Genoa, and Venice – and maps of four smaller islands, Tremiti, Elba, Corfu and Malta. The maps are based on drawings by the cartographer Ignazio Danti (1536-1586), appointed Papal Mathematician in 1580, just after having finished the Hall of Geographical Maps at Palazzo Vecchio in Florence. For the Vatican Gallery, Danti used the Apennines as a dividing line to determine where the maps should be placed on the wall. On one wall appear the regions on the Ligurian and Tyrrhenian Seas, on the other those of the Adriatic.

View of the Gallery of Maps.

Ignazio Danti
Italia antiqua
c. 1580
fresco
approx. 330 x 425 cm

The map of *Italia antiqua* (ancient Italy), on the wall of the Adriatic regions, portrays Italy at the time of the Roman Empire, in contrast to *Italia nova*, that is, sixteenth-century Italy, frescoed opposite it, on the Tyrrhenian side.

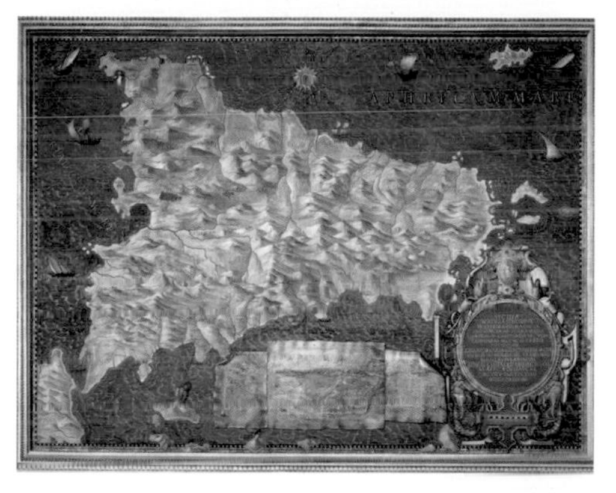

Ignazio Danti
Sicily
c. 1580
fresco
approx. 330 x 425 cm

The map of Sicily, surrounded by a sea dotted with sailing vessels and marine monsters, is accompanied by plans of its major cities, Palermo, Syracuse and Messina.

Ignazio Danti
Panoramic view of Venice
(detail)
c. 1580
fresco
approx. 330 x 425 cm

This splendid *Panoramic view of Venice*, the 'Serenissima', with its lagoon and islands also shows its inland possessions, visible in the distance.

Apartment of St. Pius V

The Gallery, the Chapel and the two small rooms, along with today's Sobieski Room, formed part of the Apartment of Pius V Ghislieri, pope from 1566 to 1572, proclaimed saint in 1712 and famous above all as promoter of the Christian coalition that decisively defeated the Turks at Lepanto in 1571. The Chapel, originally dedicated to St. Michael (the pope's secular name was Antonio Michele Ghislieri), was the pope's private chapel. All that remains of the original decoration, begun by Giorgio Vasari (1511-1574) and finished by Federico Zuccari (1540/43-1609), is the ceiling fresco depicting the Fall of Lucifer and the Rebel Angels. *The other frescoes were painted in the 19*th *century. The Gallery contains a series of tapestries of various periods and provenance, dating from the 15*th *to the 16*th *century. Among the most valuable: Episodes from the Passion, with at the centre the Last Supper (inv. 43742) and the* Tapestry of the Creed, *with the Baptism of Christ at the centre (inv. 43743), woven in Flanders in the late 15*th *century. The two rooms adjoining the Gallery (also used for temporary exhibitions) still have their original coffered ceilings with Pope Pius V's*

coat of arms in the first room and the pictorial decoration of Ferraù Fenzoni (1562-1645) and Ventura di Arcangelo Salimbeni (1567-1613) in both rooms. The first room houses a fine collection of Medieval and Renaissance Pottery coming from the Papal Palaces of the Vatican, the Lateran and the Cancelleria. The second room contains a rare and curious collection of so-called Minute Mosaics, a typically Roman art form originating in the 18th century, when Rome became a centre of primary importance for mosaic decoration (in 1727 the Vatican Mosaic Studio became a permanent institution), and for the production of mosaics commissioned of local artisans. Minute Mosaics, used mainly to decorate small personal objects, were very popular in the late 18th century and the first half of the 19th, and the pieces displayed here date from that period.

Flemish Workshop (Tournai?), *Episodes from the Passion,* second half of the 15th century; tapestry, 419 x 843 cm; inv. 43742; **Gallery of St. Pius V.**

Sobieski Room

This room, which once belonged to the Apartment of St. Pius V, is named for the enormous nineteenth-century canvas by the Polish artist Jan Matejko (1838-1893) that occupies the entire northern wall with its 41 square meters of surface area. It represents the victory won by the king of Poland Jan III Sobieski (1624-1696) over the Turks at the gates of Vienna in 1683. After the battle the Polish king wrote to Pope Innocent XI Odescalchi (1676-1689): 'Venimus, vidimus et Deus vicit *[We came, we saw, and God conquered]'. This crucially important event marked the end of the Ottoman Empire's expansion in Europe, and of the Turkish threat. To mark the bicentenary of the victory (12 September 1883) Matejko donated his painting to Pope Leo XIII Pecci. The scene of the painting being presented to the pope is depicted on the ceiling of the Gallery of Candelabra. The other paintings in this room also date from the 19th century, while some remaining fragments of a frieze are from the time of Pope Gregory XIII Boncompagni. The floor is Roman and comes from Ostia Antica.*

Jan Matejko
The Liberation of Vienna by King Sobieski
1883
oil on canvas
458 x 894 cm
inv. 42613

View of the Sobieski Room.

Room of the Immaculate Conception

The room is situated in the Borgia Tower, a new construction built for Pope Alexander VI Borgia (1492-1503) in the late 15th century during the remodelling of his private apartment in the Vatican. The frescoes, by Francesco Podesti (1800-1895), were commissioned in 1858 by Pope Pius IX Mastai Ferretti (1846-1878). In this cycle, the scenes painted on the walls are the most important. Their subject is the dogma of the Immaculate Conception, according to which the Virgin Mary was conceived without original sin. This new dogma had been proclaimed by Pius IX four years earlier, on 8 December 1854, and this room is named for it. Displayed in an imposing showcase donated by the French firm Christofle are valuable volumes, mostly manuscripts, containing the text of the papal bull translated into many different languages. They were donated to the Pope at the initiative of the French priest Marie-Dominique Sire, in 1878, by heads of State, kings, bishops, cities and dioceses. As in the Sobieski Room, the floor is Roman and comes from Ostia Antica.

View of the Room
of the Immaculate Conception.

Francesco Podesti
Proclamation
the Dogma of the
Immaculate Conception
1859-1861
fresco

Raphael's Stanze

Due to the notorious reputation acquired by Alexander VI Borgia during the last years of his pontificate, partially reassessed by historians today, his apartments were abandoned by his successor. After the very brief reign of Pope Pius III Todeschini Piccolomini lasting less than a month, from September 22 to October 18, 1503, Julius II Della Rovere was elected pope on the night of October 31-November 1 of that year. From an aristocratic Ligurian family, he was the nephew of Sixtus IV Della Rovere (1471-1484), promoter of the project for building the Sistine Chapel. The Stanza delle Sibille, according to tradition, had been the scene of a horrifying crime. Alfonso d'Aragona (1481-1500), the husband of Lucrezia Borgia (1480-1519), was murdered there at the order of his brother-in-law Cesare, known as Il Valentino (1475-1507), son of Alexander VI Borgia. By an ironic twist of fate, Cesare was later held prisoner in that same room by Pope Julius II. There was more than one reason, then, for the new pope to wish to change apartments. Accordingly, Julius II moved to the second floor, just above the Borgia apartment, in November 1507, while the rooms were still being refurbished, in premises that included not only what were to become Raphael's Stanze but also the Room of the Swiss Guards, the Sala dei Chiaroscuri, the Chapel of Nicholas V and the Logge. The first artists commissioned to embellish the new rooms included some who had participated in the decoration of the Sistine Chapel twenty years before, starting with Perugino (c. 1448-1523) and Luca Signorelli (1445-1523), along with such important additions as Piero della Francesca (c. 1416-1492), Sodoma (1477?-1549), Lorenzo Lotto (1480-1556) and others. At first they were requested to paint only the ceilings (parts of this decoration have remained) but very soon the com-

mission was extended to include the walls. The work of refurbishing the rooms in the Palace of Nicholas V Parentucelli (1447-1455) was apparently proceeding smoothly, as shown by records of regular payments made from June to October 1508, when Donato Bramante (1444-1514), the architect and painter who was supervising the project for the new St. Peter's, suggested to Julius II Della Rovere that he should put to test a young artist, Bramante's countryman. This was Raffaello Sanzio da Urbino, known to the English-speaking world as Raphael (1483-1520). Summoned to Rome from Florence where he was living at the time, Raphael immediately set to work on the studio and library of Julius II, which then become the Stanza della Segnatura, or the Tribunale, under Leo X de' Medici, although the first payments to Raphael date only from January 1509. The trial proved so satisfactory that, to their shame, all the other painters who had been commissioned to fresco the Pope's apartments were dismissed. Although some of the ceiling paintings remained, the entire decoration scheme was assigned to Raphael and his assistants. Working there from 1508 to 1524, they left one of the greatest masterpieces of the entire Renaissance, not Italian alone, endlessly praised and serving as inspiration for artists of every age (from Poussin to Ingres, from Dalí to Picasso). The visitors' route does not follow Raphael's work in chronological succession as it is described here, since the traffic flow has been changed over the years for various reasons.

View of the Stanza della Segnatura.

Stanza della Segnatura (1508-1511)

Despite the marked cultural and political differences between Alexander VI Borgia and Julius II Della Rovere, the Stanza della Segnatura reflects at least partially a theme that had already emerged in the Borgia Stanze, namely the relationship between religion and intellect, represented by a direct knowledge of Greek thought, filtered through the Neo-Platonic speculation of Marsilio Ficino and Pico della Mirandola. To this theme was added its natural complement, meditation on beauty and art as a means of arriving at Truth and God. Raphael was able to interpret these spiritual concepts and transpose them into images, giving the world such masterpieces as the *Disputa*, or *Debate over the Holy Sacrament* (1508-1509), glorifying the Eucharist and the Incarnation as the way to Salvation and Truth; the *School of Athens* (1509), representing the synthesis of Western philosophical thought with the two figures of Aristotle and Plato at the centre pointing upward and downward, indicative of reflection on the transcendent and the immanent; and the *Parnassus* (1511), which not only portrays the Muses gathered around Apollo the musician, god of beauty and art, but also hails such ancient and modern men of letters as Homer (whose features are those of the recently discovered *Laocoön*) and Dante Alighieri. This rapport with the contemporary appears in the other frescoes as well, beginning with the *School of Athens* where Raphael, tradition says, portrayed Bramante

Raphael, *School of Athens*, 1509, Stanza della Segnatura.

as Euclid, Leonardo da Vinci as Plato, and Heraclitus with the face of Michelangelo Buonarroti. The latter was added on the stairway after 1510, when Michelangelo unveiled the first part of the ceiling in the Sistine Chapel. All of this expressed the concept that Renaissance thought and ancient philosophy had been fully reconciled. The encounter, however, had taken place in the light of Christianity, as demonstrated by the *Disputa*, which glorifies the Church and Catholicism around the Host, the bread of Salvation. Here too, along with the Apostles and Fathers of the Church such as St. Augustine, we find Thomas Aquinas, Dante and Pope Sixtus IV Della Rovere. This coupling of the 'secular' and the 'religious' emerges continuously from the scenes: *Gregory IX receiving the Decretals* [canon law] and *Justinian receiving the Pandects* [civil laws] *from Tribonian*, painted in 1511 at the sides of the window. Above the latter scene is a lunette with the allegories of *Prudence* and *Temperance*, a clear admonition not to favour one side or the other excessively. On the ceiling Raphael then painted *The Judgement of Solomon* and the allegories of the Arts and Sciences (*Theology, Philosophy, Justice, Poetry*), as well as two cases of 'arrogant pride' (*ybris*) in regard to the divinity: the Biblical *Original Sin* and the mythological *Apollo and Marsyas*, who had dared to challenge the divine law of harmony. The coupling of these scenes is significant, since it legitimizes myth as an anticipation of Christian revelation.

Raphael, *Disputa*, or *Debate over the Holy Sacrament*, 1508-1509, Stanza della Segnatura.

Stanza di Eliodoro (1511-1514)

The great director of the first two rooms was undoubtedly Pope Julius II Della Rovere, inspirer of the subjects assigned to Raphael, who interpreted and transposed them into figurative language with unrivalled mastery. Here in the room where illustrious guests would be received, the subjects treated are Providence and, in particular, God's intervention in the history of mankind. Accordingly, on the ceiling, around the heraldic arms of Nicholas V Parentucelli (who was pope from 1447 to 1455) remaining from the original decoration, Raphael painted four Biblical episodes designed to be viewed in relation to those on the walls. The scene of Moses praying before the *Burning Bush* (*Exodus*, III, 1-12) surmounts, in fact, the episode that lends its name to the whole cycle (the *Expulsion of Heliodorus from the Temple*, 1511), taken from the *Second Book of Machabees* (III, 7-40). It tells the story of Heliodorus, minister to the King of Syria Seleucus IV (187-175 B.C.), who had been sent to Judea by that sovereign to confiscate the 'treasure' of the Temple of Jerusalem. Onias, the high priest, had warned him against such profanation, but in vain. Raphael depicts the culminating moment of this episode, when there appeared a 'white

View of the Stanza di Eliodoro.

Raphael, *Expulsion of Heliodorus from the Temple*, 1511, Stanza di Eliodoro.

horse with a terrible rider upon him, adorned with a very rich coverage ...Moreover there appeared two other young men... who stood by him [Heliodorus] on either side, and scourged him without ceasing with many stripes... Heliodorus suddenly fell to the ground covered with great darkness', leaving on the floor the Temple's treasure, painted by Raphael in shimmering gold leaf. Recent events had dictated the choice of this particular Biblical episode. In those very years, the Pope had managed to free Lombardy, Bologna and Romagna from French invaders. In Rome, the chronicles report, the Pope was hailed as 'never before Caesar nor any other captain', which explains his presence in the fresco. On the left, in fact, we see Julius II Della Rovere seated on the Sedia Gestatoria borne by court dignitaries, one of whom is thought to be the engraver Marcantonio Raimondi (1480-1530).
Below the *Sacrifice of Isaac*, painted on the ceiling, we find *The Miracle of Bolsena* (1512), frescoed on the south wall with the window overlooking the Cortile del Pappagallo. The problem of the window was brilliantly solved by Raphael, who designed a presbytery with stairs at the side leading up to the altar, situated between

the window and the ceiling, where the Mass is being celebrated. At its sides he painted the Pope's dignitaries attending Mass (right) and the clerics and faithful in prayer, led by the priest (left). In the miraculous episode, documented in 1263, Peter of Prague, a Bohemian priest who was celebratimg Mass in the Church of Santa Cristina at Bolsena, on Lake Bolsena in upper Lazio, saw blood exuding from the Host during the Eucharist. This miracle gave rise to the Feast of Corpus Domini, instituted on August 11, 1264 by Pope Urban IV Pantaléon (1261-1264), in which the dogma of the Transubstantiation was solemnly proclaimed. According to this dogma, the substance of bread is converted into the substance of Christ's body during the Eucharist.
On the opposite wall, with a window overlooking the Cortile del Belvedere, below the scene of *Jacob's Ladder* on the ceiling, Raphael painted *St. Peter Delivered from Prison*, one of the first nocturnal scenes in Italian art. This event in the life of St. Peter, narrated in the *Acts of the Apostles* (XII, 6-9), was divided by the artist into three episodes. At the centre, he painted the angel entering the Mamertine Prison. This strikingly effective image is one of the first backlit scenes in painting, not Italian alone. On the left appear the soldiers who, dumbfounded in the moonlight, are trying to understand what has happened. On the right, a luminous, glowing angel is leading the frightened Peter out of prison.

Raphael, *The Miracle of Bolsena*, 1512, Stanza di Eliodoro.

On the east wall, below the scene of the *Apparition of God to Noah* on the ceiling, is the fresco of *Leo the Great Turning Back Attila from Rome* (1512-1513). The pairing of the Biblical and the historical episode forcefully expresses the certainty that God will always save the just. As He acted to protect the patriarch from the great Flood, so He sent Peter and Paul to drive the Huns out of Italy. This encounter had really happened in the year 452, but on the banks of the River Mincio and not at the gates of Rome, the city visible in the background of the fresco. In this case too, the allusion is to contemporary events, here the conflict with the French, who definitively withdrew from the territories of the Church only in 1512. The following year Julius II Della Rovere died and Raphael was obliged to replace the features of Leo I the Great (440-461), originally inspired by the Della Rovere Pope, with the face of his successor: Leo X de' Medici. The rest of the scene, however, remained unchanged.

Raphael, *St. Peter Delivered from Prison*, 1512-1513, Stanza di Eliodoro.

Stanza dell'Incendio di Borgo (1514-1517)

The death of Julius II Della Rovere did not halt the decorative project for the papal apartment. Leo X de' Medici, renewing Raphael's commission, requested him to fresco another chamber. Under Julius II, the ceiling had been painted by Perugino with a representation of the Eternal, Christ, angels and the Holy Trinity. Here the wall decoration is not related to the frescoes on the ceiling, since Leo X converted into a dining room the premises where Julius II had placed the Tribunale and the ancient Stanza della Segnatura, with the Seggio appearing below the allegory of *Mercy* and *Justice*. Pope Leo X, instead, decided to concentrate on the salient facts of two of his predecessors bearing the same name, Leo III (795-816) and Leo IV (847-855), obviously interpreted in the light of current events. Accordingly, the *Fire in the Borgo* alludes to the beneficence of the pope who extinguishes the fires of war. The scene is inspired by an episode from the *Liber pontificalis*, where Pope

Raphael, *Fire in the Borgo*, 1514-1517, Stanza dell'Incendio di Borgo.

Leo IV is said to have put out the flames threatening St. Peter's by prayer alone. The Pope and the Basilica appear in the background, but accompanied by a literary citation taken from Virgil, on the flight of Aeneas, Anchises and Ascanius from burning Troy. Raphael painted the extraordinary group on the left depicting the Greek hero carrying his father on his back, with his young son beside him. Once again, however, Leo X was alluding to current events in France, as in the scene of the *Coronation of Charlemagne* in Rome by Pope Leo III, who has the face of the Medici pope, while the sovereign bears the features of Francis I of Valois, King of France (1515-1547). Unlike the *Fire in the Borgo*, painted mostly by Raphael himself, the latter fresco and others – the *Justification of Leo III* (alluding to the fact that the pope is accountable for his acts to God alone) and the *Battle of Ostia* (celebrating the victory of Leo IV over the Saracens) – were painted by Raphael's assistants, to the master's designs.

Assistants of Raphael, *Battle of Ostia*, 1514-1517. Stanza dell'Incendio di Borgo.

Stanza di Costantino (1517-1524)

The decoration of this room too continued after Raphael's death in 1520, thanks to the artistic and organisational talent of Giulio Romano. On the great south wall appears the *Battle of Milvian Bridge*, where Constantine defeated Maxentius. This fresco was painted, to a drawing by Raphael, by Giulio Romano, who also painted the *Apparition of the Cross to Constantine* on the east wall. The *Baptism of Constantine*, instead, was painted by Francesco Penni (1488-1528) who used the Lateran Baptistery as setting and gave Pope Sylvester I (314-335) the face of Clement VII de' Medici, as he did in the *Donation of Rome to Pope Sylvester*, on the wall with the windows.

Giulio Romano (to Raphael's design), *Battle of Milvian Bridge*, 1520-1524, Stanza di Costantino.

View of the Sala di Costantino with the *Battle of Milvian Bridge* by Giulio Romano, 1517-1525.

Raphael's Logge

Famed for the paintings by Raphael (1483-1520), the Logge are in fact a complex structure, formed of three orders of superimposed orders of arcades. The building, designed around 1505-1508 by the architect Donato Bramante (1444-1514), was finished only in 1519 by Raphael, who also provided for the interior decoration, in collaboration with his assistants. The first and third floors, not included in the visit, were frescoed (1560-1564) by Giovanni da Udine (1487-1564) with delicate floral patterns standing out against the sky. In the past the Logge opened onto the garden, now replaced by the San Damaso Court, and the lower loggia was open to visitors. The Loggia on the second floor, instead, was strictly reserved to the pope and his guests. Here Raphael and his assistants had occasion to display their immense talent and skill. The theme of the cycle is fully worthy of its setting and its utilisation by the pope who commissioned it, Leo X de' Medici, whose name is recorded alternatively on the trabeations of the individual aedicules: LEO X PONT. MAX. The walls were decorated by Giovanni da Udine with stuccowork, festoons of flowers and fruit and the so-called grotesques, vertical decorations copied from the underground rooms of the Domus Aurea, *the* Golden House *of Nero (64 A.D.). The ceilings of the individual bays, instead, were designed by Raphael but painted by his assistants, to his drawings. The subject is the Holy Scriptures; on the southern arcade, the thematic succession starts with* God Dividing Darkness from Light *and continues up to the* Last Supper. *The original floor, no longer present, with its decoration of lateral bands, displayed the Medicean emblems, the diamond rings and the yoke. It was laid in majolica by Luca della Robbia the Younger (1475-1548). The Logge were originally open, and the frescoes, not restored, were damaged by exposure to the weather. It was only in the years 1853-1854 that large windows were installed to protect them.*

View of Raphael's Second Loggia.

Raphael's Logge, detail of the seventh ceiling.

Sala dei Chiaroscuri

In the time of Pope Leo IX (1049-1054), a parrot, gift of the King of Denmark, flapped through the apartment after His Holiness, repeatedly squawking the name 'Pope Leo'. It is not known, however, whether the traditional name of 'parrot room' referring to the Sala dei Chiaroscuri, or Sala dei Palafrenieri, derived from the memory of this lively bird or from a lost painting of a parrot. It is instead certain that in the decoration as we see it today, the frescoes on the south wall include the figure of John the Baptist as a child, with two parrots (symbols of Christ) at his side. The room, situated on the second floor of the Apostolic Palace, is part of the medieval wing built under Pope Nicholas III Orsini. It appears today in its sixteenth-century form, distinguished by the presence of illusory decoration whose elements – statues in aedicules separated by Corinthian columns – are all imitation, giving rise to its present-day name, the Sala dei Chiaroscuri. On the cornices of the aedicules instead, frescoed like living figures, are allegorical representations of the Christian Virtues, *referring to the figures of the saints below. Hence* Continence *(gazing up toward Heaven) appears above* St. Matthew, Alms *(with a basin full of gold coins), above* St. Lawrence *and* Chastity *(with a unicorn) above* St. John the Evangelist. *Each Virtue is accompanied by an inscription in Latin; the one for this last group reads,* 'Castitatis privilegio magis dilectus', *that is 'The privilege of chastity is the greatest pleasure'. The ceiling, made by Raphael's assistants to his design, is decorated with wide, rich wooden coffers, gilded and painted, bearing the heraldic symbols of the Medici family (the three feathers, the diamond ring, the yoke and the mottoes* semper *and* suave*). The decoration was in fact commissioned, by Pope Leo X de' Medici, who held the Secret Concistory here. The room was extensively remodelled between 1558 and 1560 by the Zuccari brothers, Taddeo (1529-1566) and Federico (1540/43-1609), who restored the figures painted in chiaroscuro, destroyed during work carried out to reinforce the walls.*

View of the Sala dei Chiaroscuri.

Chapel of Nicholas V

In the Lives of the Most Excellent Painters, Sculptors and Architects *(1550-1568), Giorgio Vasari (1511-1574) recalls the project for the Chapel of Nicholas V, in his customary emphatic style: 'Fra Giovanni's fame spread throughout Italy, and Pope Nicholas sent for him, and for him Fra Angelico decorated the chapel of the Vatican Palace where the pope hears Mass with a Deposition from the Cross and some most beautiful scenes from the life of St. Lawrence'.*
'Fra Giovanni' is Giovanni da Fiesole, better known as the Blessed Fra Angelico (1395-1455), a Dominican friar already famous for having frescoed, in collaboration with Benozzo Gozzoli (1420/22-1497), the Monastery of St. Mark in Florence, where Pope Eugene IV Condulmer (1431-1447), the direct predecessor of Nicholas V Parentucelli (who was to be pope from 1447 to 1455), had stayed. Eugene IV Condulmer is thought to be the pope who summoned Fra Angelico to Rome in 1444 to fresco St. Peter's Basilica. Some scholars believe that the Chapel of Nicholas V had already been frescoed in his time, since the chronicles of the day report that, when the pope died on 23 February 1447, his body was placed 'ad cappellam parvam noviter depictam'*, that is, 'in the small newly-painted chapel'.*
However, tradition and documents concerning the laying of new flooring and the purchase of materials for the painters assign the frescoing of the 'secret chapel' (as it was also called) to Pope Nicholas V. Certainly, the cultural sphere was the same, since the decoration and the choice of artists, Fra Angelico and Gozzoli with their assistants, fell within the climate of Renaissance renewal fundamental to the programme of Nicholas V. He was in fact, the first to think of rebuilding the original Constantinian St. Peter's, replacing the old basilica with a new one inspired by Renaissance principles. He also collected the first core of the Vatican Apostolic Library, an impressive institution of culture and conservation.
The Chapel of Nicholas V is situated in the ancient tower of Innocent III, whose secular name was Lotario dei Conti di Segni (1198-1216). The tower was remodelled under Pope Nicholas III Orsini (1277-1280). Apart from the ceiling, decorated with the four Evangelists *(Luke*

View of the Chapel of Nicholas V.

*with a bull, Mark with a lion, Matthew with an angel and John with an eagle), the frescoes are devoted to St. Lawrence and St. Stephen. The latter was the first to sacrifice his life in the name of Christ, being stoned to death at the time of the Apostles outside the walls of Jerusalem (*Acts of the Apostles *VI-VII).*

St. Lawrence instead, relates the Golden Legend *(chap. CXVII) – a medieval text used as source for the frescoes – was roasted alive on a gridiron in 258, for having distributed to the poor the money from the heavy tax imposed on the Church by Emperor Valerian. Upon entering the chapel, on the upper right wall we find:* The Ordination of St. Stephen*;* St. Stephen distributing alms to the poor*; below:* The Ordination of St. Lawrence. *Entrance wall, above:* St. Stephen preaching*;* St. Stephen before the Sanhedrin*; below:* St. Lawrence receiving the treasure of the Church*;* St. Lawrence distributing alms. *Left wall, above: the* Expulsion of St. Stephen*; the* Stoning of St. Stephen. *Below:* St. Lawrence before the Emperor Decius*; the* Martyrdom of St. Lawrence. *Note that the figure of St. Sixtus, that is, Pope Sixtus II (257-258), is a portrait of Nicholas V.*

The decoration is completed by imitation fabrics bearing the coat of arms of Pope Parentucelli, figures of saints frescoed on the pillars and Giorgio Vasari's altarpiece depicting the Stoning of St. Stephen, *which has replaced the lost panel painting of the* Deposition *frescoed by Fra Angelico above the altar. The flooring is another significant element in the decoration.*

Recent studies suggest that it may allude, with the Sun at the centre and the Evangelists *on the ceiling, to the concept of the Christian cosmos as related to the zodiacal year, starting at the altar with spring, the time of the Incarnation, and continuing according to the following scheme:* Matthew, *Pisces - Aries;* Mark, *Taurus - Gemini - Cancer - Leo;* Luke, *Virgo - Libra;* John, *Scorpio - Sagittarius - Capricorn - Aquarius.*

Fra Angelico, *The Ordination of St. Lawrence*, c. 1451, Chapel of Nicholas V.

Borgia Apartment

'Having dressed as he pleased in his private chamber, the Pope went to the Sala del Pappagallo, where the Consistory was being held'. With these words Johann Burckhardt, the papal master of ceremonies better known as Giovanni Burcardo (1450-1505/6) described in his Diary *the beginning of one of the many days of Rodrigo de Borja y Doms (Rodrigo Borgia, who rose to the throne of St. Peter under the name Alexander VI). It was February 27, 1493, and work was proceeding on the still unfinished new apartments on the first floor of the old palace of Pope Nicholas V Parentucelli (1447-1455), enlarged by Pope Alexander VI with the construction of the Borgia Tower (1492-1494). Here we find some of the most beautiful frescoes in Italian fifteenth-century art, painted by Pinturicchio (1454/56-1513) with the collaboration of Piermatteo d'Amelia (1448-c. 1508), Antonio da Viterbo, known as Pastura (1450-before 1516), the Perugian artist Benedetto Bonfigli (1420-1496) and others. The frescoes were based on the studies of Giovanni Nanni, known as Annio da Viterbo (c. 1432-1502), an erudite Dominican friar. In Annio's* Antiquitates, *the relationship between Osiris and Christ is explained. Osiris is said to prefigure Christ, according to the idea, shared by Marsilio Ficino (1433-1499), that Christ's message had been anticipated in the beliefs of the* prisca religione, *a sincere, pure religion like that of the ancient Egyptians, which was to be perfected later by the coming of the Saviour. Moreover, considering that Osiris, after his death,*

View of the Sala dei Misteri.

View of the Sala dei Santi.

was born again as the ox Apis and that the bull appears on the Borgia's heraldic arms, it is clear why the Sala dei Santi is decorated with the Stories of Isis and Osiris *by Antonio da Viterbo, and Apis the ox is likened to the Borgia bull. The Borgia Apartment is a glorification of the pope and his family, the culminating point in the history of Salvation. Hence the frescoes in the Sala delle Sibille illustrate pagan predictions of the coming of Christ, written in the starry sky, with the allegories of the seven planets and their 'children', the individuals subject to their influence. In the Sala del Credo instead, the Biblical prophets announce the birth of Jesus. The Sala delle Arti Liberali expresses the capacity of the human mind to approach God through the Arts of the Trivium (Grammar, Dialectics, Rhetoric) and the Quadrivium (Arithmetic, Geometry, Music, Astronomy). In the Sala dei Santi, the same process is explained through the example of Faith, while the Sala dei Misteri is decorated by Pinturicchio with the scenes of the* Annunciation, *the* Nativity, *the* Adoration of the Magi, *the* Resurrection, *the* Ascension, *the* Pentecost *and the* Assumption of the Virgin, *that is, the mysteries of the Faith. The last Room, that of the Popes, used for solemn occasions (audiences, banquets and consistories), was frescoed with personifications of the planets known at the time, constellations accompanied by their related animals, 'grotesque' decorations by Raphael's pupil, Perin del Vaga (1501-1547), under the pontificate of Leo X de' Medici.*

Pinturicchio
Discourse of St. Catherine of Alexandria
1492-1494
fresco
Sala dei Santi

Pinturicchio
Martyrdom of St. Sebastian
1492-1494
fresco
Sala dei Santi

Collection of Contemporary Art

This collection was founded by Paul VI (Giovanni Battista Montini), pope from 1963 to 1978. In the late Fifties, a first group of modern religious works of art had entered the Pinacoteca Vaticana thanks to Pope Pius XII Pacelli (1939-1958). Encouraged by this, Montini determined from the very start to seriously address the question of relations between art and faith, an intention clearly expressed in the meeting he held with artists on May 7, 1964. He hoped that a strong, close relationship could be revived in modern times, threatened by progressive weakening of the bond that had existed in centuries past, when religion was a central theme of art and religious subjects predominated. Thanks to the unflagging efforts of Pope Paul, the Vatican's collections were soon enriched by donations from Italian and international artists, collectors, private and public institutions, creating an important repertory of modern and contemporary religious art that is still growing today. The Collection of Contemporary Art, which displays a selection of some 500 works – paintings, sculptures, prints and drawings – by outstanding Italian and international artists, with some six hundred works of art, was inaugurated by Pope Paul VI in 1973. These works are displayed in 37 rooms situated in different parts of the Vatican Palace, mainly the Borgia Apartment, where their impact is enhanced still further by the setting of rooms splendidly frescoed by Pinturicchio and his school in the late 15th century. Other modern works are displayed in the rooms below the Sistine Chapel. The leading figures in Italian art, starting from the first decade of the 20th century, include Boccioni, Balla, Carrà, De Chirico, Morandi, Rosai, and De Pisis, as well as Sironi, Casorati, Martini, Fontana, Scipione, Mafai, Cagli, Marino Marini and Manzù. Among the artists from other countries, starting from the late 19th century, are such famous names as Van Gogh, Gauguin, Matisse, Orozco, Rivera, Siqueiros, Dalí, Chagall, Kirchner, Ernst, and Bacon.

Room I in the Collection of Contemporary Art, with the gilt bronze sculpture by Lello Scorzelli (1921-1977), *Paul VI*, the pope who founded of the Vatican collection.

Room III in the Collection of Contemporary Art,
with the bust of Pope *Pius XI* by Adolfo Wildt (1868-1931).

The Chapel of Peace designed by Giacomo Manzù in 1961 and installed in the Vatican in 1973.

Vincent van Gogh
Pietà
c. 1889
oil on canvas
41.5 x 34 cm
inv. 23698

Based on a painting by Delacroix, this is one of two versions by the Dutch artist (the other is now at the Van Gogh Museum in Amsterdam).
Van Gogh (1853-1890), who moved to France in 1886, painted both versions of the *Pietà* in 1889 at the hospital of Saint-Rémy-de-Provence, where he was confined for the severe psychiatric disturbance that had led him, in December 1888, to self-mutilation (cutting off a piece of his left earlobe) after a violent argument with his friend Paul Gauguin, with whom he was living in the famous Yellow House at Arles.

The *Pietà* hints at a *pietas* felt both for the artist himself as victim of the disease, and for his neighbour in need. It expresses the deep religious sentiments always felt by Van Gogh, who before becoming an artist had wanted to be an Evangelical pastor at the service of the humble. With this spirit, he had lived for some time among the miners of a village in Borinage, Belgium, sharing their poverty and hardships and comforting them with the word of God.

Filippo de Pisis
Piazza Cavalli at Piacenza
1937
oil on canvas
60 x 80 cm
inv. 23162

Adolfo Wildt
Pius XI
1926
marble with gilding
113 x 116 x 65 cm
inv. 23660

Georges Rouault
Ecce Homo
1952
oil on canvas and panel
50 x 45 cm
inv. 23666

Marino Marini
Idea of Horse Rider
1955

polychrome plaster
225 x 100 x 250 cm
inv. 24839

Francis Bacon
Study for
Velázquez Pope II
1961
oil on canvas
150 x 118 cm
inv. 22971

Ernst Ludwig Kirchner
Lake Constance at Kreuzlingen
1917
oil on canvas
67 x 78 cm
inv. 23251

Henri Matisse
The Tree of Life
Preparatory sketch for stained-glass window in the apse

papiers decoupés
in canvas-backed paper
1949
512 x 252 cm
inv. 23757-23758

By the French painter (1869-1954), leader of the *Fauve* avant-garde movement, whose first exhibition was held in Paris in 1905, the Vatican Collection possesses the preparatory sketches 1:1 (1948-1951) for the stained glass windows in the apse of the Rosary Chapel at Saint-Paul-de-Vence on the Côte d'Azure, a major creation of his last years and one of the highest expressions of contemporary religious art. On this subject Matisse wrote: 'I want those who enter my Chapel to feel purified and lightened of their burdens [...]. This Chapel is for me the culmination of a whole lifetime of work and the blossoming of an enormous effort, sincere and arduous. It is not a work that I myself have chosen, but one for which I have been chosen by destiny near the end of my journey [...] I consider it, despite all its imperfections, to be my masterpiece [...] an endeavour that is the result of a lifetime consecrated to the search for truth'.

Salvador Dalí
Soft Monster In Angelic Landscape
1977
oil on canvas
76 x 101 cm
inv. 23719

This is one of three paintings by the Spanish artist (1904-1989) displayed in this section of the Vatican Museums. In his inimitable style, Dalí portrays the subject in a surrealist key. He remains faithful to the aesthetics distinctive of his entire artistic career, starting from his participation in the movement theorized by Breton in Paris in 1929, and despite his definitive break with the leader of the Surrealists ten years later due to conflicting ethical and political views. His dream-like images, of striking visual impact, evoke mysterious echoes in the onlooker, nourished by deformed, expanded unconscious material presenting incongruous combinations, often deliberately shocking. The painting was donated by King Juan Carlos of Spain, who granted the artist the title of Marquis of Púbol in 1982.

The Sistine Chapel

In keeping with the defensive nature of the Vatican Museums as a whole, the Sistine Chapel was designed as a building with military features, as can be seen in coeval prints and in its appearance today. Originating as the Palace Chapel of Sixtus IV Della Rovere, it was built starting in 1477 and was completed on August 9, 1483, anniversary of the Pope's election, when the first Mass was celebrated there. Records of payments show that the Chapel was built by Giovannino de' Dolci (1435-1486), although he may have been the contractor rather than the architect, considering that it was most probably designed by Baccio Pontelli (1450-1494/95).

The Chapel was built in the vicinity of the ancient Sala Regia, in place of the Palace Chapel of the medieval building, encapsulating some of its wall structure. It measures slightly over 40 x 13 meters, and is nearly 21 meters high. These dimensions, undoubtedly stipulated by the pope, have the same proportionate relationship as those of both Noah's Arc, the Old Testament symbol of the Church, and Solomon's Temple. They follow the numerical succession of 6 x 2 x 3, where, taking 1 as unit of measurement, the first number refers to the length, the second to the width and the third to the height. However, the great hall as it appeared to Sixtus IV's contemporaries differed from the one we see today.

Most notably, the Ceiling did not yet display the frescoes of Michelangelo Buonarroti (1475-1564). It was decorated instead with an elegant star-strewn sky of gold against a blue background painted by Piermatteo d'Amelia (1448/50-1503/8), whose project is now in the Uffizi (Gabinetto dei Disegni e delle Stampe).

And of course the *Last Judgement* painted by the great Tuscan master did not yet exist. In its place were two windows, in line with those of the side walls. The Sistine Chapel was not devoid of paintings, however, since pope Sixtus IV had summoned the most famous artists of the time to decorate it. The cycle of frescoes included, and to a large extent still includes, a succession of popes and the *Events from the Life of Moses* confronted with *Events from the Life of Christ*, as natural complement to the Old Testament.

Only the two short walls have been transformed, beginning with the east wall, where Michelangelo painted the *Last Judgement*. Before this, at the height of the windows, the decoration continued with false niches containing representations of the popes and, most probably, the figure of Christ, founder of the Church.

View of the Sistine Chapel.

View of the side wall of the Sistine Chapel.

St. Peter and his first two successors, St. Linus and St. Cletus, all painted by Perugino (1448/50-1523) must have come next. Perugino also painted the great scenes of the *Nativity of Christ* and *Moses Rescued from the Waters*. Of all this, nothing has remained, apart from the drawing, done by memory, of the *Assumption of the Virgin* (Vienna, Albertina), a copy after Perugino.
The presence of this fresco was linked to the dedication of the chapel, consecrated to the Virgin Mary by the Della Rovere Pope. Below the paintings, then as now, was the imitation *Velarium*, the fresco adorning the lower register of the Chapel, painted to emulate a damasked fabric in yellow and white, the papal colours, to

which were added the heraldic emblems of Sixtus IV, the wild oak, and the papal insignia. A nineteenth-century print (1899; now in Florence, Casa Buonarroti) by Gustavo Tognetti shows how the chapel, elegant and majestic, must have looked in the late 15th century.
Running from the north to the south side of the Chapel, on the long sides, are representations of the popes, ranging from St. Peter to St. Marcellus, who occupied the papal throne from 296 to 304. Starting from the first, they are: Anaclete (north wall, NW); Clement (south wall, SW); Evaristus (SW); Alexander (NW); Sixtus I (SW); Telesphorus (NW); Hyginus (SW); Pius (NW); Anicetus (SW); Soter (NW); Eleutherius (SW); Victor (NW); Zephyrinus (SW); Calixtus (NW); Urban (SW); Pontianus (NW); Anteros (SW); Fabian (NW); Cornelius (SW); Lucius (NW); Stephen (SW); Sixtus II (NW); Dionysus (SW); and Felix (NW). On the east wall are four more figures: Caius, Eutychianus, Marcellinus and Marcellus.
This passing from the north to the south wall is the key to interpreting the whole cycle, since it represents a comparison between the Old and the New Testament, the former being seen as prefiguring the latter. Accordingly, looking away from the *Last Judgement*, we find all of the *Events from the Life of Moses* on the right (south wall) and all of the *Events from the Life of Christ* on the left (north wall). The scenes facing each other intensify the significance of the relationship between the events of the Old and the New Testament. The hinge point consisted of the lost *Moses Rescued from the Waters* and the lost *Nativity of Christ,* painted behind the altar and destroyed in 1534 to make room for the *Last Judgement*. Today instead the first episode on the right depicts *Moses and his Wife Sephora Returning from Egypt to Free the Hebrews*. Next comes the *Circumcision of the Sons of Moses,* painted by Pietro Perugino with the collaboration of Pinturicchio (1454-1513). This scene is divided into two episodes inspired by the passage in *Exodus* (IV, 19-21, 24-26) relating how, at the order of Yahweh, Moses Returns to Egypt to Free the Hebrews. It is in these circumstances that Yahweh appears before Moses, intent on killing him, wrathful that the patriarch has neglected to have his sons circumcised; however, his wife Sephora immediately performs the circumcision, as shown by the scene on the right.
The episodes described above were painted after those by Botticelli (1445-1510) appearing in the next scene. The theological advisers decided to present them first in order to match the *Baptism of Christ*, painted by Perugino, on the opposite wall, thus emphasizing the link between Baptism and Circumcision, and the importance of each to its own religion.
Next come Botticelli's frescoes depicting *Moses Defending the Daughters of Jethro* and *The Burning Bush*, datable between 1481 and 1482, illustrating the episodes from the *Life of Moses* narrated in the first verses of *Exodus*. To the right appears the scene (II, 11-12) of the *Slaying of the Egyptian* and the *Flight of Moses*. At the centre we find *Moses Defending the Daughters of Jethro* (II, 17); above it is the famous scene of *The Burning Bush* (III, 2-6) and to the left, the *Exodus of the Hebrews from Egypt* (III, 12, 17-18). Next comes the *Crossing of the Red Sea*, painted during those same years by Biagio di Antonio Tucci (1466-1515).
At this point the episodes depicted in the frescoes return to their natural chronological succession. The grandiose scenes assume an almost surreal tone in the literal translation of such narrative details as the colour of the sea – red, as it appears in the geographical maps of the time – and the column rising at the centre

Sandro Botticelli, *Moses Defending the Daughters of Jethro*; *The Burning Bush*, 1481-1482.

Biagio di Antonio Tucci, *Crossing of the Red Sea*, 1481-1482.

of the fresco. This is a visual image of the column of clouds and fire (*Exodus*, XIV, 19-22) that protected the Hebrews on their journey to the Promised Land. The scenes of *Moses on Mt. Sinai* and the *Adoration of the Golden Calf* painted in 1482 by Cosimo Rosselli (1439-1507) have been appropriately placed in relation to Jesus' *Sermon on the Mount* on the opposite wall, also by Rosselli. This fresco il-

Cosimo Rosselli, *Adoration of the Golden Calf*, 1482.

Sandro Botticelli, *Punishment of Korah, Dathan and Abiram*, 1482.

lustrates the episodes described in *Exodus* (XX-XXXIV) with special emphasis on Moses receiving the tablets of the Ten Commandments (XX, 1-17). Below, the artist depicts the *Descent from the Mountain with the Tables of the Law*, the *Adoration of the Golden Calf* (XXXII, 1-8) and *Moses Breaking the Tables of the Law* (XXIII, 19); note, below, the presence of a monkey, symbol of the devil.

The *Punishment of Korah, Dathan and Abiram*, frescoed by Sandro Botticelli in 1482, should be compared with the scene of *Christ's Charge to St. Peter*, painted by Perugino on the opposite wall. The Biblical episode, taken from the *Book of Numbers* (Chapter XVI), depicts the rebellion of Korah, Dathan and Abiram who, along with many others, questioned the authority of Moses and his brother Aaron. Botticelli enriched the scene with references to antiquity and to Rome, placing the Arch of Constantine and the Septizonium of Septimius Severus in the background. The figures grouped to the right in the background are portraits of fifteenth-century notables. Still in 1482, Luca Signorelli (1445-1523) and Bartolomeo della Gatta (1448-1502) painted the fresco with the scenes: *Moses Gives his Staff to Joshua, Distribution of the Promised Land to the Tribes of Israel*, and the *Death of Moses*. The common theme of these episodes is the naming of Moses' spiritual heir. This concept should be seen in relation to *Christ's Charge to St. Peter* on the one hand, and the *Last Supper* by Rosselli and Biagio di Antonio on the other, since the Eucharist, instituted at the Last Supper, may be considered a distribution of Christ's spiritual legacy. Signorelli's fresco was inspired by the events related in *Deuteronomy* (Chapters XXXI-XXXIV), where Moses names Joshua, a courageous soldier of proven worth, his successor (XXXI, 7-8). Although the Biblical text does not describe how this took place (except by a reference to the imposition of the hands, which may be metaphorical: XXXIV, 9), the consignment of the staff is an allusion to the destiny of Joseph, chosen to be Mary's husband.
The right wall of the Sistine Chapel begins at the end with the *Baptism of Christ* (1482), painted by Perugino's assistants with the uncertain contribution of Pinturicchio. In this fresco the figures are dressed in fifteenth-century costume, making the scene topical, while in the background appears an ideal Jerusalem, so closely resembling Rome that it even has a Colosseum. This is followed by the double

Sandro Botticelli, *Temptation of Christ*, 1482.

Domenico Ghirlandaio, *Calling of the First Apostles*, 1482-1483.

scene of the *Purification of the Leper* and the *Temptation of Christ*, painted by Botticelli in 1482. The relationship between this fresco and the one facing it – depicting the episodes of the *Burning Bush* and the *Trials* endured by Moses to reaffirm his Hebrew dignity – express the concept of purification implicit to resisting temptation, and to the 'healing of the leper', who is now dressed in white as required by Jewish custom, according to the *Book of Leviticus* (Chapter XIV). Entirely consistent with this concept is the allusion to Christ as 'physician' of the body and soul, expressed in the image of the Santo Spirito Hospital in Sassia, the architectural glory of Pope Sixtus IV. This fresco may also contain portraits of high-ranking members of the papal court such as Giuliano della Rovere, the future pope Julius II, and Girolamo Riario (1443-1488), nephew of Sixtus IV.
Next comes the *Calling of the First Apostles*, painted by Domenico Ghirlandaio between 1482 and 1483. It is based on passages from the *Gospels* of Matthew (IV, 18-22), Mark (I, 16-20) and Luke (V, 1-11). In the background appears the scene of the miraculous catch of fish, identifying the lake behind them as Gennesaret. The link with the Old Testament consists of the element water, present also in the *Crossing of the Red Sea*, painted by Biagio di Antonio, where the enemies of Israel are destroyed by the sea. In the miraculous catch of fish instead, the lake symbolizes life and abundance for those who have been touched by the word of Christ.
The next fresco, depicting the *Sermon on the Mount* and the *Healing of the Leper*, was painted by Cosimo Rosselli in 1482. The 'sermon on the mount' is the central episode in Christ's preaching. On this occasion He laid the foundations of Christianity, based on piety and compassion. It is thus a new Ten Commandments, a new Table of the Law; hence this episode is related, in the Sistine Chapel's iconographic programme, to the scenes of *Moses on Mt. Sinai* and the *Adoration of the Golden Calf*, also painted by Rosselli. The 'sermon on the mount' is reported in detail on-

Pietro Perugino, *Christ's Charge to St. Peter*, 1482.

Cosimo Rosselli and Biagio di Antonio Tucci, *Last Supper*, 1481-1482.

ly in Matthew (V-VII) and Luke (VI, 17-49), while the 'healing of the leper' is mentioned also in Matthew (VIII, 1-4) and Mark (I, 40-45). In Luke (V, 12-14) this episode is reported as occurring before the 'sermon on the mount'.
The most famous fresco in the cycle is, however, *Christ's Charge to St. Peter*, painted by Pietro Perugino in 1482. This episode, reported by Matthew (XVI, 19), constitutes a real investiture, sanctioning Peter's supremacy over all the other Apostles. On a deeper level, however, this scene is related to the *Punishment of Korah,*

Dathan and Abiram, painted by Botticelli. In the background appear two episodes frescoed by Perugino: on the right, the famous *Tribute to Caesar* (*Matthew*, XXII, 15-22; *Mark*, XII, 13-17 and *Luke*, XX, 20-26), on the left the *Attempt at Stoning Jesus*, an event mentioned in the text of John (VIII, 59; X, 31-39). This scene should be viewed as counterpart to the choice of Peter and in relation to Jesus' words: 'The stone that the builders discarded / has become the cornerstone' (*Luke* XX, 17).
The image in the background created by Perugino and his theological consultants clearly expresses the idea that the 'stone' discarded from the Temple is Christ, understood by neither the priests nor the faithful. That 'stone' will become the keystone of the new edifice of faith that is the Church, whose foundation is Peter and whose 'cornerstone' is Christ.
The wall concludes with the *Last Supper* painted by Cosimo Rosselli with Biagio di Antonio in 1482. In the background to this scene the artist and the advisory theologians wisely chose to depict scenes from the Passion of Christ: at right, the *Prayer in the Garden*, at centre the *Capture of Christ* and on the left the *Crucifixion*. Appearing below is the scene of the *Last Supper*, with Judas seated on the other side of the table in accordance with long tradition. Below, the scene of a dog and a cat fighting is clearly a metaphorical image of the clash between good and evil.
The west wall (with the entrance to the Chapel), facing the *Last Judgement*, collapsed in 1522 at the time of Pope Hadrian VI Florenszoon Boeyens (1522-1523). It was rebuilt and decorated with new frescoes by Hendrick van den Broeck (1519-1597), the *Resurrection of Christ*, and Matteo da Lecce (1547-1616), *The Archangel Michael Defending the Body of Moses*, in 1571-1572.
It is here that the artistic and intellectual journey of Michelangelo Buonarroti begins. We need only look upward to admire the incomparable masterpiece of the Ceiling painted by him and justly hailed by Giorgio Vasari (1511-1574) as 'the lantern of our art'. This work has had, in fact, an enormous influence on figurative art, from

Michelangelo, *Erythraean Sibyl* (left) and ***Delphic Sibyl*** (right)**, 1508-1511.**

Michelangelo, *Libyan Sibyl* (left) and ***Persian Sibyl*** (right)**, 1508-1511.**

Taddeo Zuccari to Eugène Delacroix, from Johann H. Füssli to David Lachapelle, and even on the cinema and advertising of today. Moreover, as can happen only with great artistic phenomena, even its degradation has served as inspiration for painters. When newly painted, with its dazzling colours (rediscovered in the restoration conducted from 1980 to 1989), the Ceiling was undoubtedly the inspiration for sixteenth-century Mannerist painting.
Much later, when it had been darkened by dirt and smoke from candles, it inspired the romantic artists of the 19th century. Commissioned of Michelangelo by Pope Julius II Della Rovere, the nephew of Sixtus IV, for whom the Chapel had been built,

Michelangelo, *Prophet Zachariah* (left) and ***Prophet Ezekiel*** (right)**, 1508-1511.**

Michelangelo, *Judith and Holophernes*, 1508-1511.

the great project of the Ceiling distracted the master from his previously accepted task of designing and sculpting the papal *Tomb of Julius II*. The artist, at first reluctant to accept the commission, then threw himself into this work that absorbed all of his energy from 1508 to 1512, with an interruption lasting from September 1510 to August 1511, rarely descending from the scaffolding and painting even by candlelight.
From here, Michelangelo began to paint after a long series of studies and preliminary drawings to define the composition of the Ceiling, designed as an architectural structure with lowered arches linking the benches of the *Sibyls* and the *Prophets* placed at the sides of the spandrels. In comparing *Zachariah*, above, (symbol of Christ's entry into Jerusalem as well as the Pope's entry into the Sistine Chapel) with *Jonah* (symbol of resurrection and hence placed above the altar), painted four years later, a marked difference in style can be seen in the two figures. While the first figure sits immobile on his marble throne, the other seems to be bursting out of his chair. Although the tradition of the Sibyls and Prophets was widespread in the Middle Ages and the Early Renaissance (they appear, in fact, on the floor of the Siena Cathedral, as well as in the Borgia Stanze), Michelangelo instilled them with new life, transforming them into Titans.
The four corner pendentives of the Ceiling are decorated with Biblical episodes taken from the history of Israel. To the left of *Zachariah* is the scene of *Judith and Holophernes*, with the Biblical heroine cutting off the head of the Assyrian commander (*Judith*, XIII, 6-11), while to the right, in *David and Goliath*, the future King of Israel slays the Philistine champion in the same manner (*First Book of Samuel*, XVII). At the end, to the left of *Jonah*, appears the episode of the *Bronze Serpent* erected by Moses in the desert (*Numbers*, XXI, 9) and on the opposite side the *Punishment of Aman*, the cruel, ambitious adviser to the Persian king Assuerus who planned to kill all of the Hebrews deported to Persia, but was hanged himself instead (*Esther*, VII, 1-10).

Michelangelo, *Drunkenness of Noah*, 1508-1511, Ceiling.

Michelangelo, *Sacrifice of Noah*, 1508-1511, Ceiling.

Michelangelo, *Flood*, 1508-1511, Ceiling.

On the spandrels and in the lunettes Michelangelo represented the genealogy of Christ, with special attention to the maternal lineage, deemed more important than the paternal, which is frequently subordinated to the female ancestors. This choice may have been complementary to the necessarily male genealogy of the popes, to be considered almost a gallery of kings. What is certain is that Michelangelo retained in the lunettes and the spandrels the same kind of comparative reading that, from the altar, extends to the west wall.
Above the *Prophets* and *Sibyls*, seated on the marble blocks of the cornice bordering the central area, are the famous *Ignudi*, nude figures alluding to humanity prior to the Revelation, according to symbolism already employed by the master in the *Doni Tondo* (c. 1506-1508). Their positions are determined by their frustrated desire to know God. Their shoulders are draped with garlands of oak leaves, the emblem of Julius II, in celebration of the new golden age inaugurated by the pope. The *Ignudi*, which have served as model for painters and sculptors of every age, from Caravaggio to Bernini, from Rodin to Klimt, are flanked by imitation bronze shields and medallions decorated with Biblical scenes taken from the *Book of Kings*.
In the great central rectangle, with its marble arches and cornices, appear scenes ranging from the *Drunkenness of Noah* to the *Separation of Light and Darkness*, all episodes taken from the *Book of Genesis*. This is, however, the chronological

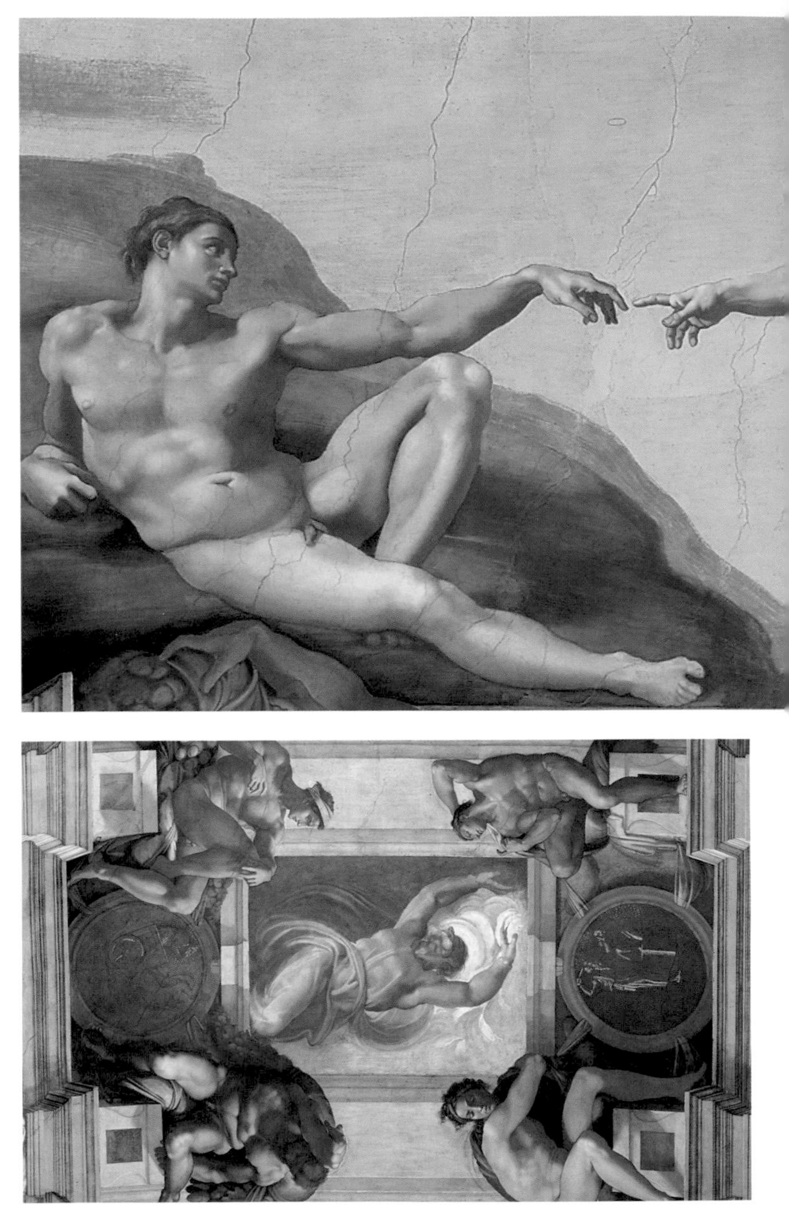

Michelangelo, ***Separation of Light and Darkness*****, 1508-1511,** Ceiling.

Michelangelo, *Creation of Adam*, 1508-1511, Ceiling.

succession of the work (since the artist started from the west wall), but not the narrative sequence, which begins instead at the altar. As regards formal aspects, the scenes become progressively simplified and the personages fewer in number. The first episodes, such as the *Drunkenness of Noah*, the *Sacrifice of Noah* and the *Flood* (1508-1509), have a choral dimension that becomes increasingly monumental in scenes such as the *Creation of Adam*, the most famous in the whole cycle – the model for Mannerists such as Pellegrino Tibaldi (1527-1596) as well as for advertisements such as the one for a French liqueur appearing in 1987 – the *Creation of Eve* and the *Original Sin*. In the *Separation of Light and Darkness*, the *Creation of the Heavens* and in the *Separation of Land from Water*, the only protagonist is God, whose figure is sometimes repeated twice.

The *Last Judgement*

The history of the Sistine *Last Judgement* is long and tormented. It was painted over the span of seven years and two pontificates (from its commissioning in September 1534 to All Saints' Day of 1541, when the Chapel was inaugurated). Commissioned, in fact, by Clement VII de' Medici (1523-1534), it was completed under Paul III Farnese (1534-1549). Careful examination of the work shows that the artist drew inspiration for the composition from the painting of northern Europe, known to him through the *Judgement* by Buonamico Buffalmacco (doc. 1315-1336) in the Camposanto at Pisa.
Recent studies have called attention to the fact that the *Last Judgement* was influenced by Platonic spec-

Michelangelo, *Christ the Judge*, 1536-1541, detail of the *Last Judgement*.

Michelangelo, *Last Judgement*, 1536-1541.

ulation on the countenance of God, known to Michelangelo through the commentary of Marsilio Ficino (1433-1499) to Plato's *Convivium*, and the *De visione Dei* of Nicola Cusano (1401-1464). Deep reflection on this subject appears in many of Michelangelo's poems, where he considers the countenance of God to be the origin of all others, the uncreated mould for the faces of men, which reflect it with varying degrees of beauty and harmony.
The literary sources for the *Last Judgement* include not only the *Divine Comedy* of Dante Alighieri (1265-1321) and the *Apocalypse*, but also the *Iudicium Dei* (1508) by Giovanni Sulpicio da Veroli, who was master of Latin rhetoric to Alessandro Farnese, the future Pope Paul III. The references to this text are so many and so strong as to leave little room for doubt, as, for instance, in the description of the central group with *The Virgin* and *Christ the Judge*: 'At the centre, glowing with light, more resplendent than the sun, will appear Christ with Mary, Virgin and Mother, whose brilliance will outshine the moon and stars'.

Michelangelo, ***Group of the Saved*** and ***Exaltation of the Instruments of the Passion*** (opposite page, above and at centre), **1536-1541, details of the *Last Judgement*.**

Michelangelo, *Caron Ferrying the Souls of the Damned to Hell*, 1536-1541, detail of the *Last Judgement*.

Then, continues Sulpicio, Christ 'with a tremendous gesture' (*gestuque tremendo*) will judge the good and the evil. In this incomparable scene, 195 figures rotate around the Saviour, who has the resplendent features of the *Apollo Belvedere* (130-140 A.D.), while the Blessed rise at his right and the Damned fall at his left. Below them is Hell, with Caron ferrying the Damned on his boat along the River Styx to meet Minos; above appear angels with trumpets, and above them, in the lunettes, the heavenly messengers bearing the instruments of the Passions.

Michelangelo, *Minos, judge of the Underworld*, 1536-1541, detail of the *Last Judgement*.

Michelangelo, *Angels with Trumpets and Books of Judgement* (above) and *St. Peter* (below), 1536-1541, details of the *Last Judgement*.

Museums of the Vatican Library

Although the Library's Museums have been included in the Vatican Museums only since 1999, the history of their formation is almost as long as that of the Church. Starting from the territorial organization of the first dioceses, in fact, the earliest Christian communities – and that of Rome in particular – kept local archives to conserve their memories. Throughout the Middle Ages and part of the Renaissance, the place designated to safeguarding these documents was the sacratissimum Lateranensis palatii scrinium, *the ancient residence of the popes in the Lateran and seat of the Apostolic Chancellery from the time of Julius I (337-352). Near the end of the 15th century, an important part of the papal records was moved to Castel Sant'Angelo, where an archive was set up under Sixtus IV Della Rovere (1471-1484). In the 14th and 15th centuries such humanist popes as Boniface VIII Caetani (1294-1303), Nicholas V Parentucelli and Sixtus IV Della Rovere strongly encouraged the founding of a real library collection. It is to Sixtus IV that we owe the official Bull of Foundation of the library (15 June 1475). This historic event is commemorated by Melozzo da Forlì in a famous fresco (c. 1477) now in the Vatican Pinacoteca, depicting the conferring of the title of Prefect on the humanist Bartolomeo Sacchi, known as Platina (1421-1491). In the following centuries, with the*

View of the Salone Sistino.

transfer of the seat to the sixteenth-century wing of the Palaces, the imposing collections being accumulated by the library in the areas assigned it grew to include – in addition to library materials proper – articles of archaeological, and more specifically decorative importance, such as cameos, coins, glassware, seals, gemstones, bronze statuettes and goldwork, antiquarian collector's items complementary to the interests of erudite research. In the 19th-20th century the collections incremented in this way were subjected to radical reorganization and many objects collected in the past migrated to new destinations. Noteworthy among the rooms in today's Museums of the Library is the nineteenth-century Room of Tributes, or Sala degli Indirizzi, so-called for having housed, under Benedetto XV Della Chiesa (1914-1922) the objects indirizzati, *that is, 'addressed' to the popes by Catholics from all over the world. Here are displayed silverware, enamels, vestments, reliquaries, crucifixes and objects made of ivory, documenting the wide-ranging tendencies favoured over the centuries by papal patronage. The Room of the Aldobrandine Wedding, decorated by Guido Reni in 1608, is named for the great wall painting from the Augustan Age perhaps depicting preparations for the wedding of Alexander the Great and Roxana. The eighteenth-century Room of the Papyri, with paintings of allegorical subject by Anton Raphael Mengs (1772-1773), houses a precious selection of terracotta works by Bernini. The Sacred (or Christian) Museum, founded in 1756 by Pope Benedict XIV Lambertini (1740-1758), displays varied materials coming from the Roman catacombs: glassware, tableware, oil lamps, coins, cameos, seals and ancient silverware. The Salone Sistino and the two Sale Sistine commemorate the name of Sixtus V Peretti (1585-1590), who, between 1588 and 1590 had the rooms embellished with frescoes dedicated to the history of books and the salient facts of his own pontificate. The cupboards standing in interminable rows along the walls of the Pauline Rooms, the Alexandrine Room and the Clementine Gallery, whose walls are also decorated, recall the functions served by these rooms before the books were brought here. The Profane Museum, created by Pope Clement XIII Rezzonico (1758-1769) at the northern end of the Galleries, has housed since 1767 a fine collection of Etruscan and Roman antiquities comprising inscriptions, gemstones, mosaics, and sculptures in bronze, bone and alabaster.*

View of the Museo Sacro (or Christian Museum).

Pinacoteca

The Vatican Pinacoteca boasts over 500 paintings, spanning the history of art in the western world from the 12th to the 19th century. Originating as a picture gallery set up in the late 18th century during the pontificate of Pope Pius VI Braschi, it occupied the corridor known today as the Tapestry Gallery. The first core collection, consisting of a hundred or so paintings, was progressively enriched by purchases and donations. In addition, the so-called Primitives and the Byzantine icons were moved here from the Vatican Library, while other masterpieces were brought from the altars of St. Peter's Basilica and the Lateran Pinacoteca. The idea of a modern museum, open to the public, had arisen already in 1817, after the paintings confiscated in Napoleonic times had returned from France, but the present-day Pinacoteca was opened only in 1932, when Pope Pius XI Ratti commissioned Luca Beltrami (1854-1933) to provide the definitive project. In part of the nineteenth-century Square Garden, the architect designed a building composed of a series of Renaissance-style rooms. The paintings are displayed in eighteen rooms, arranged chronologically and according to the various schools and subjects: I. Primitives; II. School of Giotto and Late Gothic; III. Fra Angelico, Filippo Lippi, Benozzo Gozzoli; IV. Melozzo da Forlì, Marco Palmezzano; V. Various 15th century masters; VI. Polyptychs; VII. 15th century Umbrian School; VIII. Raphael; IX. Leonardo and other 16th century artists; X. Titian and 16th century Venetians; XI. Later 16th century artists; XII. Baroque; XIII. 17th and 18th century; XIV. Various subjects; XV. Portraits; XVI. Paintings by Wenzel Peter. The last two rooms display bronze sculptures (XVII. Bernini's models) and the collection of icons (XVIII. Byzantine icons).

Wenzel Peter
Adam and Eve in the Garden of Eden
c. 1830
oil on canvas; 336 x 247 cm
inv. 41266
Room XVI

The great canvas by Wenzel Peter (1745-1829), who specialised in painting flora and fauna, was purchased by Pope Gregory XVI Cappellari in 1831, along with 19 other works by the Bohemian artist, to decorate the Sala del Concistoro in the Papal Apartment. Today it is displayed in Room XVI along with some of Peter's paintings done in Rome.

Nicolò and Giovanni
Last Judgement
signed 'Nicolaus et Johannes'
second half of the
12th century
tempera on panel
288 x 243 cm
inv. 40526
Room I

Coming from the Oratory of San Gregorio Nazianzeno in Rome, this great round painting with its rectangular base depicts the *Last Judgement* in a very rare format, enlivened by the vivacious narrative style typical of Roman painting.
The scenes, accompanied by explanations in writing, are arranged in superimposed registers; from the top: Christ in Majesty; the Redeemer with the Apostles; Saint Paul with the Elect; the Virgin with Saint Stephen and some Works of Mercy; the Resurrection of the Dead; the Heavenly Jerusalem, and Hell.
The painting must have been donated by the Abbess Costanza and the nun Benedetta, portrayed at bottom left, at the feet of the Virgin praying among the Elect in Paradise.

Giotto and assistants
Stefaneschi Triptych
front and back
(below, right, detail
of the donor Stefaneschi)
c. 1320
tempera on panel
178 x 89 cm (central panel),
approx. 168 x 82 cm (side panels),
45 x 83 cm (each section
of the predella)
inv. 40120
Room II

The *Stefaneschi Triptych* marks an important stage in the artistic maturity of Giotto di Bondone (1267-1337), who painted it, with his assistants, around 1320.
Of notable historic value as well, it was commissioned by the Roman Cardinal Jacopo Caetani degli Stefaneschi (1270-1343), one of the most erudite, influential figures of his time. For him, Giotto also painted a fresco, now lost. Stefaneschi, appointed canon of St. Peter's Basilica under Pope Celestine V Angeleri da Morrone (1294) and named cardinal deacon of San Giorgio al Velabro under Boniface VIII Caetani (1294-1303), was the author of numerous texts, including a biography of Celestine V and a report on the First Jubilee held in 1300.
Commissioned for the high altar in the first St. Peter's Basilica, the old Constantinian church, the painting was later moved to the Sacristy. It was painted on both sides, front and back, so that it could be seen by the clergy behind the altar as well as the faithful in the naves. On the front, facing the congregation, appears *St. Peter*

Enthroned with Angels. Kneeling at his feet are the cardinal offering the triptych, presented by St. George, and Pope Celestine V, already wearing the halo of a saint (he was canonized in 1313), presented by St. Sylvester, offering a manuscript. In the side panels appear *St. Andrew and St. John the Evangelist* (right) and *St. James and St. Paul* (left). On the surviving panel of the predella, *Three saints* are portrayed half-length.

On the back appears *Christ Enthroned with Angels and Cardinal Stefaneschi*; on the side panels, the *Crucifixion of St. Peter* (left) and the *Beheading of St. Paul* (right). On the predella, divided into three panels, are the *Virgin and Child Enthroned with Two Angels and the Twelve Apostles*.

Real objects such as the pyramid of Caius E. Cestius in Rome, near Porta Ostiense, are depicted in the painting, but as regards stylistic traits, the figures lack the weight and volume characteristic of Giotto's paintings, indicating the participation of his assistants.

Gentile da Fabriano
St. Nicolas revives three children found cut up in pieces in a barrel
(predella panel from the *Quaratesi Polyptych*)
1425
tempera on panel
36.5 x 36.5 cm
inv. 40250
Room II

This panel is one of four in the Pinacoteca coming from the predella of the *Quaratesi Polyptych* depicting *Stories of St. Nicholas* (the fifth is in the Washington National Gallery). The main panels of the polyptych are instead in the Galleria degli Uffizi, Florence, and the National Gallery, London.
A lost inscription stated that the work, painted for the Quaratesi family chapel in the Church of San Niccolò Oltrarno, Florence, was finished in May 1425.
Painted while Gentile da Fabriano (*c.* 1375-1427) was staying in Florence, the polyptych was thus done after the *Adoration of the Magi* for the Florentine banker Palla Strozzi (1372-1462), finished in 1423 (Florence, Uffizi), that is, two years prior to the artist's death in Rome. For their lively, expressive style, the predella panels are the real masterpiece of this polyptych. In the one shown here, along with the three revived children emerging from the barrel are such striking details as the mezzanine filled with barrels and hanging strands of garlic, the view of the courtyard and, half-hidden, the customer at the table.

Fra Angelico
Stories of St. Nicholas of Bari (Birth of St. Nicholas; His vocation and the alms to the three poor girls; Meeting with the emperor's messenger; Miracle of the grain and the miraculous saving of a sailing ship)
panels from the predella of the *Guidalotti Altarpiece*
c. 1437-1445
tempera and gold on panel
35 x 61.5 cm (right panel), 35.5 x 64.4 cm (left panel)
Room III

These two panels come from the predella of the altarpiece painted by Fra Angelico (c. 1395-1455) for the Guidalotti Chapel in the Church of San Domenico in Perugia (the rest of the polyptych is now at the Galleria Nazionale dell'Umbria in Perugia). It is dated at either 1437 – reported by a 16th century chronicle as the year it was painted – or 1447, when Pope Nicholas V Parentucelli, sometimes identified with the figure of St. Nicolas, was elected. The splendid seascape in the predella depicting the *Tempest and the Miracle of the Grain* is thought to have been drawn by Fra Angelico, but painted by the refined Florentine artist Zanobi Strozzi (1412-1468), who frequently collaborated with the older master.

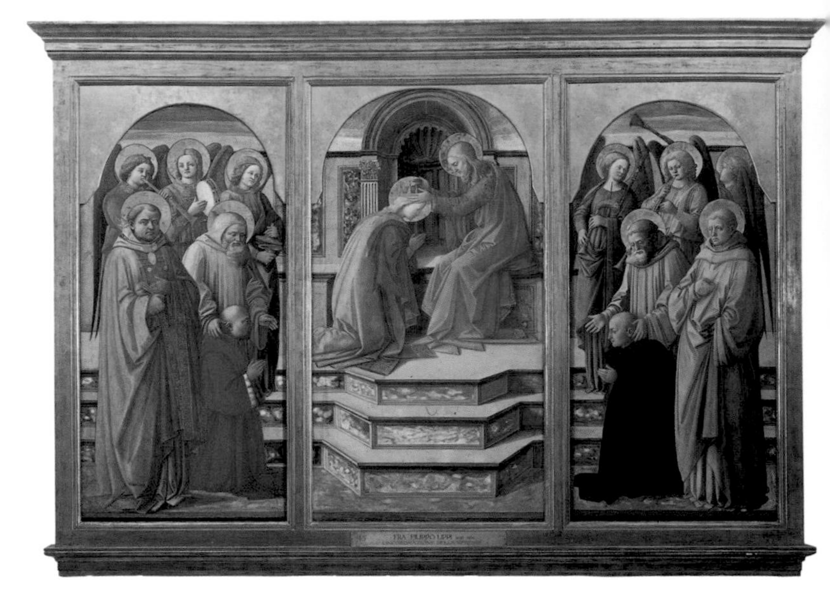

Filippo Lippi
***Coronation of the Virgin, Angels, Saints and the Donors* (*Marsuppini Coronation*)**
c. 1444-1445
tempera and gold on panel
170 x 95 cm (central panel), 164 x 83 cm (side panels)
inv. 40243
Room III

The subject of the altarpiece by the Florentine painter Filippo Lippi (1406-1469) is the *Coronation of the Virgin*, an event that takes place in Heaven (patches of blue sky can be seen) but is, however, depicted at the top of an elegant, realistic polychrome marble tier of stairs. The Virgin and Christ are flanked by musical angels above, with the saints and donors below. The work was commissioned by Carlo Marsuppini (1399-1453), secretary of the Republic of Florence, for the Chapel of St. Bernard in the convent of Olivetan nuns at Arezzo, and donated in 1444, at the death of Gregorio Marsuppini, father of the donor and brother of Laurentino, Governor General of the Olivetan Congregation.
In the right-hand panel, the man kneeling in prayer is probably Carlo Marsuppini, while the figure shown genuflecting on the left has been identified as his father Gregorio. The saints portrayed are linked to the Congregation of the Olivetans: at left, standing, is St. Gregory the Great, at right the Blessed Bernardo Tolomei (1272-1348), the Sienese abbot who founded the Congregation. The figures dressed as monks, protecting the donors, are most probably St. Benedict and St. Bernard. Originally, the altarpiece was a single panel, which may have had a predella.
The style is more austere than in other similar paintings by Filippo Lippi, perhaps because the work was painted for a convent, and with the participation of assistants.

Benozzo Gozzoli
The Virgin shows her Child to St. Thomas (Madonna of the Girdle)
1452
tempera and gold on panel
133 x 164 cm (central panel)
inv. 40262
Room III

This altarpiece was painted against a gold background in 1452 by the Florentine artist Benozzo Gozzoli (1421-1497) for the high altar of the church of San Fortunato at Montefalco, in the Province of Perugia. In 1848 it was donated by the Umbrian Commune to Pope Pius IX Mastai Ferretti, who had it placed in the Pinacoteca of the Lateran Palace; it was moved later to the Lateran Pinacoteca. The Virgin is shown surrounded by angels, handing St. Thomas the girdle that the Apostles had bound around her waist after her death. This is one of the Florentine master's most interesting paintings, distinguished by delicate, luminous colours and refined botanical details. In the predella, episodes from the Life of Mary – the *Birth of the Virgin*, the *Betrothal*, the *Annunciation*, the *Nativity*, the *Circumcision*, and the *Passing Away of the Virgin* are beautifully illustrated. In the tomb filled with flowers at the Virgin's feet is an opening that appears to have been used for communicating with cloistered nuns.

Melozzo da Forlì
Sixtus IV and Platina
1477
detached fresco,
transferred to canvas
370 x 315 cm
inv. 40270
Room IV

This fresco, which originally decorated a room in the Latin Library, founded in 1474 by Sixtus IV Della Rovere, is the work of the painter from Romagnolo Melozzo da Forlì (1438-1494), who moved to Rome in 1475 to pursue a successful career at the papal court.

Important for historical reasons, the fresco is also an elegant exercise in painting Renaissance architecture in perspective, viewed slightly foreshortened from below, representing real-life personages. Pope Sixtus IV is shown appointing the humanist Bartolomeo Sacchi, known as il Platina (1421-1481), first prefect of the Vatican Library. Platina is shown kneeling at the centre, pointing to a humanist inscription he has composed.

The other figures are the Protonotary Apostolic Raffaele Riario (1480-1521), nephew of Cardinal Giuliano della Rovere, the future Pope Julius II, Girolamo Riario (1443-1488), nephew of Pope Sixtus IV, and Giovanni della Rovere (1457-1501).

Melozzo da Forlì
Head of Apostle
and *Musical Angels*
c. 1480
fragments of fresco
various sizes
invs. 40269.14.3; 40269-14.9; 40269-14.6; 40269-14.5
Room IV

The fourteen fragments of the *Apostles* and the *Musical Angels*, as well as the *Blessing Christ* (now in the Palazzo del Quirinale), come from the *Ascension of Christ*, a fresco (destroyed in 1711) in the apse of the Basilica dei Santi Apostoli in Rome. The fresco dates from around 1480, a time subsequent to the remodelling of the basilica carried out under Cardinal Giuliano della Rovere, the future Pope Julius II.

Here Melozzo da Forlì, at the height of his artistic maturity, displays all of his talent in the foreshortened and perspective views of the Apostle's heads and the serene figures of the musical angels.

Antonio Vivarini
St. Anthony the Abbot and other Saints
signed and dated 1464
carved and painted wood (the statue),
carved and gilded frame;
tempera and gold on panel
105 x 130 cm (lower panels),
80 x 50 cm (upper central panel),
53 x 30 cm (side central panels)
originally in the Church of Sant'Antonio
a Pesaro, then in the Lateran Pinacoteca
inv. 40303
Room VI

Giovanni Bellini
Pietà
c. 1471-1474
oil on panel
107 x 84 cm
from the *Pesaro Altarpiece*,
formerly in the Church
of San Francesco a Pesaro
inv. 40290
Room IX

The *Pietà* was originally the gable of a masterpiece by the Venetian artist Giovanni Bellini (*c.* 1432/33-1516), the *Pesaro Altarpiece* (now at the Museo Civico in Pesaro). The panel, taken to Paris by the French in 1797, was returned to Rome in 1816. With its extraordinary foreshortened figures against the background of a deep blue sky strewn with clouds, the painting represents the dead Christ, his body resting on the edge of the tomb, his legs projecting forward toward the spectator, supported by the monumental figures of Mary Magdalene, Nicodemus and Joseph of Arimathea.

Raphael
Madonna of Foligno
c. 1511-1512
tempera grassa on panel, transferred to canvas
308 x 198 cm
originally in the Church of Santa Maria d'Ara Coeli in Rome, then in the Church of the Convent of Santa Anna delle Contesse in Foligno
inv. 40329
Room VIII

Commissioned in Rome from the young Raffaello Sanzio, known as Raphael (1483-1520), by the humanist nobleman from Foligno Sigismondo dei Conti (1432-1512), this work is an *ex voto* depicting the donor genuflecting, presented by St. Jerome to the Virgin in heaven with her Child, seated on luminous clouds and surrounded by little angels. At his home in Foligno, Sigismondo had escaped being struck by lightening. This scene appears in the background of the landscape, in perfect harmony with the gentle, serene figures in the foreground. On the left are St. John the Baptist and St. Francis.

Musei Vaticani
Bookshop Desk 1 3
00120 Citta Vaticano

Ricevuta del Titolare

Transazione
Visa Contactless
Visa Credit
XXXXXXXXXXXXX6799

20.04.2015 11:57:01
Trm Id: [illegible]
Contatore Trx: 17001

Totale EFT EUR 12.00

Aduno payment services
www.aduno.ch

Raphael
Transfiguration
1517-1520
tempera grassa on panel
410 x 279 cm
originally in the Church of San Pietro in Montorio in Rome
inv. 40333
Room VIII

This great altarpiece represents, above, the episode of Christ on Mount Tabor. Jesus appears transfigured before his disciples, flanked by the prophets Elijah and Moses in heaven. Below, the Apostles are trying to help a child possessed by devils, supported by relatives imploring their assistance. The monumental figures in the foreground are a dramatic match for the equally spectacular scene of the Transfiguration. The painting was commissioned in 1515 by Cardinal Giulio de' Medici, the future Pope Clement VII, who planned to donate it to the Cathedral of Narbonne in France, but after the artist's death it remained in Rome.

Leonardo da Vinci
St. Jerome
c. 1482
oil on panel
103 x 75 cm
inv. 40337
Room IX

The destination of this rare painting by Leonardo da Vinci (1452-1519) is unknown. He left it in Florence, in the state of unfinished monochrome, when he departed for Milan in 1482. The survival of this work, which was owned for some time by the Swiss painter Angelica Kauffmann (1741-1807) in Rome, is almost miraculous. It was found, in fact, by Cardinal Joseph Fesch (1763-1839), Napoleon Bonaparte's uncle, in disastrous conditions. The head was being used as the seat of a stool, and the rest as the lid of a coffer. In the background, to the right, is a sketch of the Florentine Church of Santa Maria Novella.

Titian
Madonna of San Niccolò del Frari
signed by the artist
c. 1533-1535
oil on panel
388 x 270 cm
inv. 40351
Room X

Painted for the Church of San Niccolò della Lattuga in the Campo dei Frari in Venice, this altarpiece (whose arched upper part has been lost), a work from the maturity of Titian (1488/90-1576), portrays the Virgin on a cloud, looking downward at the monumental figures of Saints Sebastian, Francis, Anthony of Padua, Peter, Nicholas, and Catherine of Alexandria.

Caravaggio
The Deposition
c. 1604
oil on canvas
300 x 203 cm
originally in the Church
of Santa Maria in Vallicella,
Rome
inv. 40386
Room XII

The masterpiece of the Vatican Pinacoteca was painted in Rome in 1604 by Michelangelo Merisi, known as Caravaggio (1571-1610), at the request of Girolamo Vittrice, who placed it in the family chapel at the Church of Santa Maria in Vallicella (also known as Chiesa Nuova) to honour the memory of his uncle Pietro, who died in 1600. It depicts the moment when Christ is deposed from the Cross, his body laid on a great stone to be washed and anointed with perfume. The figure of Christ was clearly inspired by Michelangelo's *Pietà* in St. Peter's Basilica.

Guido Reni
Crucifixion of St. Peter
c. 1604 1605
oil on panel; 305 x 171 cm
originally in the Church
of San Paolo alle Tre Fontane
inv. 40387. **Room XII**

The painting dates from the beginning of the Roman sojourn of Guido Reni (1575-1642), a native of Bologna. It was painted around 1604, commissioned by Cardinal Pietro Aldobrandini (1571-1621) for the Church of San Paolo alle Tre Fontane. It was moved to the papal palace at the Quirinal in 1787, taken to Paris in 1797, and lastly, placed in the Pinacoteca of Pope Pius VII Chiaramonti in 1819. Here Reni shows himself attentive to the innovations of Caravaggio. Although his canvas has the same subject as Caravaggio's painting done for Santa Maria del Popolo in 1601, his style remains more classic and less dramatic.

Gregorian Profane Museum

The museum was founded by Pope Gregory XVI Cappellari, who installed a substantial number of ancient sculptures and relief carvings in the Lateran Palace in 1844, where they remained until the 1960s. They were moved to their current seat in the Vatican Museums (along with the collections of the Pio Christian Museum and the Ethnological Missionary Museum) by Pope John XXIII Roncalli. The inauguration took place in 1970. The museum is divided into various sections, distinguished by an arrangement that is not only rigorous but also light, airy and easy to understand.

View of the Gregorian Profane Museum.

Head of Athena

c. 460 B.C.
Southern Italy
marble
h. 44.5 cm
inv. 905
Section II

This is a fragment of an acrolith, a statue whose parts are made of different materials. The head and hands were usually made of marble or ivory (or metal), and the rest of less precious, less durable materials, often wood covered with metal leaf. The technique was widely used in Greece. In this case, the eyeballs are made of semiprecious stone, while the pupils (lost) must have been made of vitreous paste. The holes in the head were for attaching a helmet, and earrings hung from the ears.

Bearded head

448-432 B.C.
from Athens
marble
h. 19.2 cm
inv. 1013
Section II

This head is one of a group of three fragments coming from the decoration of the Parthenon in Athens, the Greek city's greatest temple, built by Iktinos under Pericles and decorated with sculptures by Phidias between 448 and 432 B.C. The head, presumed to represent the legendary King Erechtheus, comes from one of the temple's 92 metopes, the slabs adorning the band above the columns, in this case on the south side. The metopes on the Parthenon formed a series depicting the primordial struggles between gods and heroes to establish world order.

Horse's head

448-432 B.C.
from Athens
marble; 26.2 x 65,3 x 24.5 cm
inv. 1016
Section II

This fragment too comes from the Parthenon in Athens, specifically from the decoration on the west pediment, illustrating the contest between Athena and Poseidon. This head belonged to a horse that was harnessed to the goddess's 'quadriga'.

Fragment of mosaic floor

1st-2nd century A.D.
from Rome
405 x 405 cm
inv. 10132
Section III

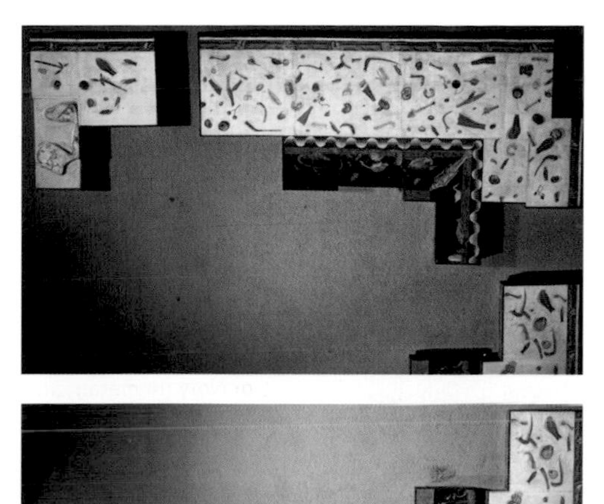

The two surviving concentric portions of lateral bands around the floor – found in a private residence on the Aventine Hill – display two decorative motifs: a scene of life on the banks of the Nile, against a dark background, and an *asaroton*, a curious decoration simulating an 'unswept floor' covered with the remains of a meal. The decoration also includes a row of six tragic masks.

Poseidon

1st-3rd century A.D.
Roman copy
of a Greek original
marble
h. 216 cm
inv. 10315
Section II

This colossal statue represents the god of the sea, Poseidon (Neptune), his foot resting on the bow of a ship, with a dolphin.

Athena (left)
plaster cast; h. 149 cm
inv. 37022

Marsyas (right)
marble; h. 171 cm
inv. 9974

1st-2nd century A.D.
Roman copy
of Greek original
Section I

The two figures echo a famous composition in bronze by the Greek sculptor Myron (5th century B.C.).
The scene represents the first step in the tragic story of the Silenus Marsyas, a river god, who picks up the double flute Athena has just thrown to the ground.
The goddess strikes Marsyas in anger, but later he begins to play the flute, and so well that he challenges Apollo to a contest, the cithara against the flute.
The god wins and punishes Marsyas for his arrogance by tying him to a tree and flaying him.

Tiberius
1st century A.D.
from Cerveteri
marble
inv. 9961
Section VII

The seated statue portrays the emperor who succeeded Augustus and reigned from 14 to 37 A.D., wearing a wreath of oak leaves, a tribute awarded to persons of outstanding civic virtue in the Roman world.

at bottom:

Altar of the Vicomagistri
30 40 A.D.
from Rome
marble
invs. 1156, 1157
Section VII

These two slabs probably do not belong to a sacrificial altar, but to the base of a monument from the time of Tiberius (14 B.C.-37 A.D.) or Claudius (41 A.D.-54 A.D.). The decoration represents a sacrificial procession, with two consuls, two lictors, some musicians, the three animals to be sacrificed, veiled youths and personages wearing togas, low-ranking officials responsible mainly for public ceremonies, the 'Vicomagistri', were district authorities in the city of Rome. The reliefs come from the ancient Campus Martius.

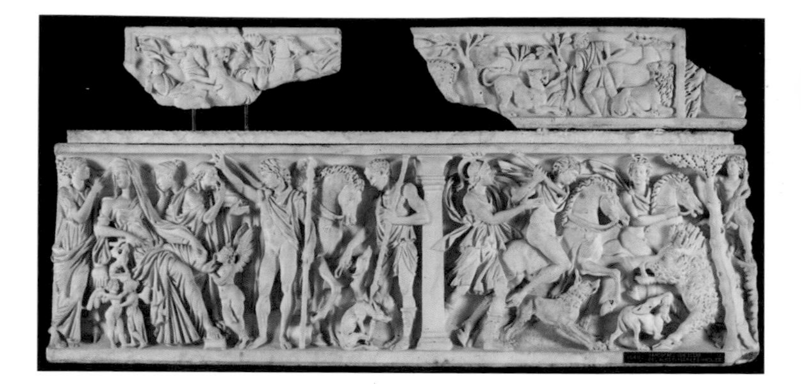

Sarcophagus with scenes of Phaedra and Hippolytus
c. 220 A.D.
from Rome
marble
63 x 191 x 69 cm (body)
h. 29 cm (lid)
inv. 10400
Section XIII

The decoration on the sarcophagus tells the story of Phaedra, the wife of Theseus who falls in love with her son-in-law Hippolytus. In the version of the tragedy given by Euripides (480-406 B.C.), this happens due to a spell cast by Aphrodite. Phaedra, overcome with passion, tells her nurse, who then reveals everything to Hippolytus. When he resentfully abandons the city, Phaedra commits suicide, leading Theseus to believe she has been violated by her stepson. Theseus invokes Poseidon, and Hippolytus too meets with death, before the grief-stricken Theseus discovers the truth too late.

Sarcophagus with scenes from the Myth of Adonis
c. 220 A.D.; from Rome
marble
inv. 10409
Section XIII

The scenes illustrating the myth of Adonis narrate the death of the beautiful youth beloved by Aphrodite. He is killed by a wild boar, sent by the jealous Ares, while hunting. Aphrodite then managed to keep him with her for at least part of the year.

The Ephesian Artemis
2nd-3rd century A.D.
(original head;
body extensively
restored in the 17th century)
from Rome
marble
h. 187 cm (statue)
h. 22 cm (head)
inv. 10410
Section XVI

The cult of the goddess Artemis was so strong and deep-rooted throughout Asia Minor that, for St. Paul, it formed one of the greatest obstacles to the spread of Christianity. The figure of Artemis assumed varying connotations in different cultures and at different epochs. The Roman Diana, goddess of the forest, differed in some respects from the Greek Artemis – goddess of the hunt – while the Middle Eastern divinity (the Ephesian Artemis), with her many rows of animal testicles, was a kind of Earth Mother who nourished all creatures and ensured fertility.

Pio-Christian Museum

The works displayed in the Pio-Christian Museum, like those of the Gregorian Profane Museum – with which it shares the premises designated in the 1960s by Pope John XXIII Roncalli and Pope Paul VI Montini – come from the Lateran Apostolic Palace, where they had been placed by Pope Pius IX Mastai Ferretti, founder of the museum, in 1854. Most of the objects displayed here come from the catacombs and early Christian churches of Rome. Forming a collection unique the world over, they consist mainly of early-Christian sarcophagi, dating from the 3rd to the 5th century. The exhibition is completed by an epigraphic section (Christian Lapidarium) with important inscriptions, mainly funerary, along with epigraphs found in the Jewish catacombs of Monteverdi (Jewish Lapidarium). The objects displayed in the Pio-Christian Museum document the crucial moment when a clearly Christian iconography began to emerge from the roots of classic Graeco-Roman art, assumed and reinterpreted in natural manner to present the contents of a new faith.

The Pio-Christian Museum portrayed by Filippo Cretoni on a cabinet in the Vatican Library, 1857, Vatican Museums, first Sala Sistina.

The Good Shepherd
c. 300 A.D.
from Rome, Catacombs
of San Callisto
marble; h. 100 cm
inv. 28590

The iconography of the shepherd carrying a lamb (or a ram) on his shoulders was already widespread in the ancient world. In early Christianity it gradually came to personify the figure of Christ, 'the Good Shepherd, who gives his life for his sheep' (*John*, X, 11). This sculpture shows all of the characteristic traits of classic realism. The face is inspired by the figure of the God Apollo, chosen by the early Christians to represent the visual aspect of Jesus. What appears as a statue today was originally part of the decoration adorning the front of a monumental sarcophagus, restored and integrated in the form of a statue in the 18th century.

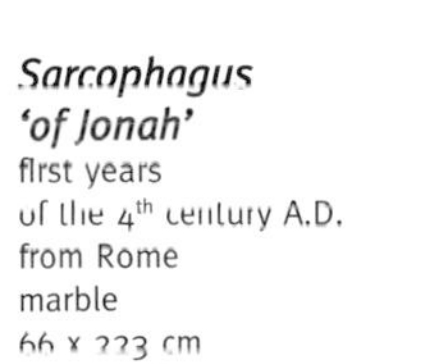

Sarcophagus 'of Jonah'
first years
of the 4th century A.D.
from Rome
marble
66 x 223 cm
inv. 31448

The so-called *Sarcophagus 'of Jonah'* is one of the Museum's masterpieces, with its dramatic representation of the prophet thrown overboard and swallowed by a sea monster, then saved by God and washed up on the shore, and lastly resting under the tree that has miraculously sprung up to shade him. This is the earliest example, dating from before the Peace of Constantine, of a sarcophagus decorated almost exclusively with Biblical scenes.

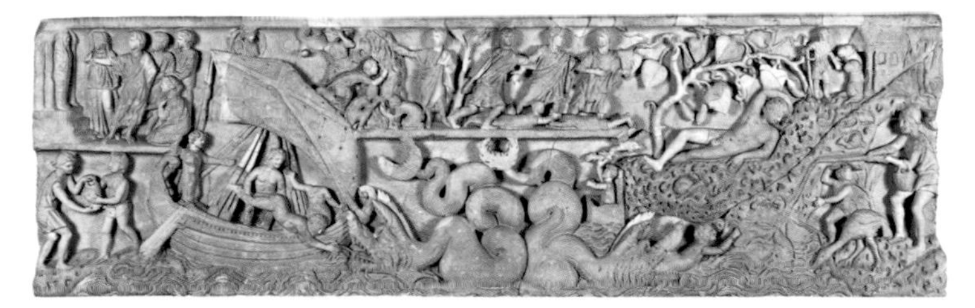

Sarcophagus of 'Two Brothers'
first half
of the 4th century A.D.
from Rome
marble; 113 x 213 x 121 cm
inv. 31543

This sarcophagus is named for the double portrait of two men appearing at the centre of one of the long sides. The rest of the decoration depicts episodes from the New and the Old Testament. The sarcophagus was found in the vicinity of the Basilica of San Paolo fuori le Mura (St. Paul's outside the Walls).

Sarcophagus with the 'Crossing of the Red Sea'
late 4th century A.D.
from Rome
marble
57 x 223 x 68 cm
inv. 31434

The decoration evokes the famous Biblical episode narrated in the *Book of Exodus*: the people of Israel, led by Moses, flee from Egypt, crossing the Red Sea, whose waters open miraculously when Moses holds over them the staff God has given him, closing again instead to engulf the enemy in pursuit, led by Pharaoh. This is the first time, nearly a hundred years after the *Sarcophagus 'of Jonah'*, that a Biblical episode occupies the entire front of a sarcophagus, a true example of the Word in images.

'Dogmatic' Sarcophagus
330-340 A.D.; from Rome
marble; 131 x 267 x 145 cm (body); 30 x 273 x 148 cm (lid)
inv. 31427

This sarcophagus has two bands of decoration. In the upper band, at the centre, is the portrait of a husband and wife; to their left are scenes of the creation of Eve and the consigning of the symbols of work to our first ancestors, while some of Christ's miracles are represented on the right. In the lower band, starting from the left, appear scenes of the Adoration of the Magi; the healing of the blind man; Daniel in the lions' den and stories of Peter (the prediction of his denial, his arrest and the baptism of his jailers). The sarcophagus is called 'dogmatic' for its many references to the dogmas proclaimed at the Council of Nicea, 325 A.D. We can recognize – in the three personages shown in the act of creating Eve, on the upper left – the most ancient attempt to portray the mystery of the Trinity, with the Father seated on his throne in the 'creator' gesture of the word and the Son, who is in fact the Logos/Word of God 'by means of whom all things have been created'. The style, with the figures more elongated and less harmonious (those of the Magi, for instance), as compared to the nobler tone of the *Sarcophagus of 'Two Brothers'*, shows a more modern current of Constantinian art, a prelude to medieval developments.

Philatelic and Numismatic Museum

The Vatican City State has been a sovereign nation since 1929, when the Lateran Treaty between the Holy See and the State of Italy was signed. Formally, the Vatican City State could be called an elective absolute monarchy. Like every other nation, the Vatican has a currency, the Euro, and issues postage stamps. The museum, in the modern arrangement completed in 2007, displays the Vatican's philatelic and numismatic production issued by the Vatican City State from 1929, but including coins and stamps from the earlier Papal State – as well as sketches, plates for engravings, and medals – offering a sort of journey through time over the last two centuries.

Missionary Ethnological Museum

The Missionary Ethnological Museum was set up subsequent to the Universal Missionary Exhibition, held in the Vatican Gardens under Pope Pius XI Ratti during the Holy Year of 1925. Organised to greet pilgrims with a spectacle of art and spirituality, the 1925 Exhibition made the work of missionaries known throughout world, while at the same time attracting over a million visitors with a display of more than 100,000 objects from widely differing cultures, specially selected and sent by missions in the Far East, Oceania, North and South America and Africa. At the close of the Exhibition, whose notable scientific value was apparent to all, Pope Pius XI decided to display the ethnographic collections on a permanent basis, founding a museum for them that was inaugurated in December 1926. A special commission chose some 40,000 of the most significant pieces; objects from the Borgiano Museum of the Propaganda Fide and from private collections were soon added.
The new museum, occupying two floors of the Lateran Palace, was transferred to its present seat in the Vatican Museums at the initiative of Pope John XXIII Roncalli, and was inaugurated in 1973 during the pontificate of Paul VI Montini. The collection, containing abundant documentation on non-European cultures and religions, boasts a number of objects unique the world over. Many of the works, moreover, bear witness to the spread of Christianity through the work of missionaries.

Japanese art
Portable Kodansu
late Edo Period
1615-1867
lacquered wood
with gold dust
12 x 9.3 x 18.4 cm
inv. 126364
Asia Section, Japan

Polynesian art
The god Tu
The god Rongo
before 1836
carved wood
from Mangareva,
Gambier Archipelago
(French Polynesia)
invs. 100189, 100185
Oceania Section, Polynesia

The two statuettes of Tu and Rongo, divinities in the Polynesian pantheon, are among the rare surviving examples of the art of woodcarving on Mangareva, a little island in the Gambier Archipelago, southeast of Tahiti. They were shipped to Europe by missionaries in 1836, as a record of the local cults that had been supplanted by Christianity.
Only a few examples of this kind exist in the whole world, produced by the artist/priests (*taura-rau*) of Mangareva. Tu, god of warfare and destruction, is portrayed with four legs and human feet. The surface of his body is carefully polished, as is the statuette of Rongo (literally, 'sound'), whose aspect is more realistic. Rongo was the god of peace and cultivated plants, the bringer of rain and rainbows.

Tambaran
(Initiation hut)
early 20th century
replica with various objects
Oceania Section,
New Guinea

The section devoted to New Guinea is exceptionally important for the rarity of the objects, most of them sent in 1925 and 1932 by the Divine Word Missionaries, which document the culture of the peoples inhabiting the regions around the River Sepik. The initial core collection was formed by Father Franz Joseph Kirschbaum S.V.D., missionary and anthropologist, the first occidental to reside, in the early 20th century, in those still unknown lands.
This hut, reconstructed using original pieces from central New Guinea, holds great historic and scientific value for the information it provides on the customs of the Sepik peoples. It is a ceremonial hut, dedicated to the cult of ancestors, reserved exclusively to adult men. Here painful rites of initiation were practiced, as shown by the numerous instruments exhibited inside the hut, along with other ritual objects.

Replica of pre-Columbian Breastplate with anthropo-zoomorphic figures
20th century
(copy of an original
from the 9th century A.D.?)
brass
h. 29.4 cm
inv. 121761
South America Section,
Colombia

The *Breastplate* forms part of the rich collection of objects (vases, fragments, sculptures, gold jewellery) from South America, followed by collections from Central America, bearing witness to the cults existing before the conquest of these regions by European nations.

Art from the Solomon Islands
Madonna and Child
20th century
painted wood
160 x 35 x 38 cm
inv. 112773
Oceania Section, Melanesia

This statue portrays a Madonna and Child with the dark skin typical of the Melanesian peoples. Her short, upswept hairstyle resembles a helmet of curls. Dressed only in a pareo covering her thin body, she holds the little Jesus clutched to her breast. The holy figure is adorned with a necklace drawn on her skin and circular tattoos on the arms, below the knees and on the ankles.
This singular sculpture seems to have been commissioned from a craftsmen in the Solomon Islands by a missionary bishop, to decorate the cathedral of one of the islands in the archipelago.
The missionaries from the Western World, however, struck by the marked realism of the image, deemed it improper to display the statue in church. Today, this fascinating work is recognised as a testimonial to the process of 'enculturation' of the peoples converted to Christianity, that is, the translation of Christian symbols into their own artistic and symbolic language.

Luba Art
Kifwebe (Mask)
20th century
hardwood with white
and plant fibre incisions
37.5 x 15 x 16 cm
inv. 101064
Africa Section,
Democratic Republic
of Congo

For the Luba, the *Kifwebe* ceremonial mask, representing a female figure and used only by women in dances to the moon, holds various symbolic meanings. The colours and differing arrangement of the incisions in the face allude to such animals as the lion, the zebra, the crocodile and the porcupine.

Art of
South-East-Asia
Singa
(Mythological creature)
19th-20th century
Bali
carved and painted wood
inv. 100113
Asia Section,
Indonesia

According to an ancient tradition, widespread throughout South-East Asia, Balinese temples were decorated with sculptures portraying mythological creatures, as protection for the worshippers. One of these was Singa, a winged mythological figure, represented here by a vivacious painted wooden statue coming from the Island of Bali.

Carriage Museum

The Carriage Museum is a branch of the Historical Museum housed in the Papal Apartment of the Apostolic Palace at the Lateran. Founded by Pope Paul VI Montini in 1973, the Carriage Museum occupies a vast area (105 x 14 meters) under the so-called Square Garden. The collection consists of the historic means of transportation – from the sedan chair to the carriage to the automobile – used by the various popes, with their equipment and accessories, as well as documentary material of various

kinds. The museum's main attraction consists of the nineteenth-century carriages, strikingly arranged along both sides of the room. At the centre is the 'Gran Gala' berlin *of Pope Leo XII della Genga (1823-1829), with major modifications by Pope Gregory XVI Cappellari (1831-1846). Red like all of the papal carriages and decorated with wood and gilt metal inlays, it had to be drawn by six horses, and was used only four times a year for papal visits (prescribed by protocol) outside of Vatican City.*

'Gran Gala' Berlin
of Pope Leo XII, with modifications of Pope Gregory XVI
1824-1826; 1841
wood
320 x 600 x 240 cm,
375 cm (shaft)
inv. 45551
Carriage Museum

Vatican Gardens

'Bellica Pontificis non fundit machina flammas / Sed dulcem belli qua perit ignem aquam' *('The Pope's war machine launches no flames, but rather the sweet water that extinguishes the fire of war'). With these Latin verses, Pope Urban VIII Barberini praised the extraordinary play of water offered by the* Fountain of the Galley. *The gilt bronze ship, in fact, sprays water from its cannons. This gave the great pope, who often composed verses on works of art (his distich for the* Apollo and Daphne *of Gian Lorenzo Bernini, 1621-1623, is famous), a chance to express the hope for peace that has always been pursued by the Holy See. The Fountain, unfortunately, is not accessible to the public during the guided visits to the Vatican Gardens organized by the Museums. The Gardens cover some 22 hectares, half the total extension of the tiny Vatican State. The need of Gardens for repose and meditation was first felt by Pope Nicholas III Orsini (1277-1280) when he abandoned the Lateran Patriarchate, moving to a new seat on the Vatican Hill beside the* tomb of St. Peter.

The idea for the Gardens thus arose in 1279, and the formal act establishing their borders is kept at the Palazzo dei Conservatori al Campidoglio, in the Sala dei Capitani. In reading the epigraph, it can be seen that the original layout was that of a medieval garden, since the pope specified that it should consist of a pomerium, *or fruit orchard, a* pratellum, *or lawn, and a* viridarium, *a garden proper that also contained medicinal herbs. Of this original core, nothing has remained; in its place are the various buildings and courtyards of the Vatican Museums. What has survived, however, is the concept of a cool retreat, a place for meditation and a relationship with the sacred that has developed progressively over the centuries. Here we find, in fact, a replica of the* Grotto of Lourdes, *donated by French Catholics to Pope Leo XIII Pecci in commemoration of the apparition of the Virgin to the young Bernadette Soubirous in 1858. The sacred nature of the place is also expressed by the* Chapel of the Madonna della Guardia, *with a replica of the statue of Mary that overlooks the entry to the port of Genoa, donated by the citizens of that city to Pope Benedict XV Della Chiesa (1914-1922).*

Shaded by trees in the English garden stands the statue of St. Peter in Chains, *sculpted in 1887 by Amalia Dupré (1842-1928), the first work of art by a woman to be welcomed into the Vatican State. The Gardens also have a naturalist dimension, where all of the diverse fashions and philosophies of garden architecture live together in harmony: from the Italian garden with its formal geometric motifs created from boxwood hedges and ornamental flowers, to the English landscape garden where nature appears to grow in total spontaneity, to the rose garden whose arches covered with roses frame a view of the dome of St. Peter's in the distance. Water plays from monumental works (all fed from Lake Bracciano) like the* Fountain of the Eagle, *designed*

and built by Jan van Santen (1550-1621), better known as Giovanni Vasanzio, who also created the Fountain of the Sacrament, *so called because its jets of water resemble a monstrance surrounded by six candles.*
The Gardens are adorned by buildings that are real architectural jewels, such as the 'Casina' of Pius IV *(Giovan Angelo de' Medici, 1559-1565) built between 1558 and 1561 by Pirro Ligorio and seat of the Pontificia Accademia delle Scienze (Papal Academy of Science).*

View of the Vatican Gardens.

Vatican Grottoes

'To whom coming, as to a living stone, rejected indeed by men, but chosen and made honourable by God. Be you also as living stones built up, a spiritual house...' This passage from the First Epistle of St. Peter *(II, 4-9), which had a vast echo among the exegetes and commentators of the Holy Scriptures starting with St. Augustine, is the best key to correctly interpreting the significance of the Vatican Grottoes, or Tombs of the Popes. Here the bodily testimony of each pope may be considered a 'living stone' that contributes to building the spiritual edifice which is the Church. Starting under Gregory XIII Boncompagni (1572-1585) and continuing under Clement VIII Aldobrandini (1592-1605), burial places were built here for the popes, cardinals and sovereigns deemed particularly worthy by the Church. At the heart of the radial central section is the* Niche of the Palliums, *standing exactly over the* tomb of St. Peter. *The pallium is a liturgical vestment worn specifically by the pope. It is*

View of the Vatican Grottoes.

a stole woven from the white wool of two lambs blessed by the pope, marked by six crosses embroidered in black silk (red in the Middle Ages). Today, the right to wear the pallium may also be granted to Metropolitan Archbishops. Palliums blessed by the pope are kept in the silver urn placed on the tomb of St. Peter *at the centre of the Niche. The Grottoes, however, are also a place of historic and artistic memory. Here we find, for example, the* Angel *coming from the now lost mosaic of the* Navicella *made by Giotto for the ancient façade of St. Peter's Basilica; and the mosaic thought to be part of the tabernacle in the Oratory of Pope John VII (705-707); as well as the two marble* Angels *from the funerary monument of Boniface VIII, carved by Arnolfo di Cambio. The Vatican Grottoes are entered from inside St. Peter's Basilica, passing through the entrance at the* Pillar of St. Longinus, *or outside, from Largo Braschi, through an access designed to accommodate the disabled.*

Antonio Canova and **Adamo Tadolini,** ***Statue of Pius VI,*** detail, 1821-1822, **Vatican Grottoes**

St. Peter's Basilica

'You are Peter and on this rock I will build my Church, and the gates of Hell shall not prevail against it. I will give you the keys of the kingdom of heaven, and whatever you bind on earth shall be bound in heaven, and whatever you loose on earth shall be loosed in heaven' (*Matthew*, XVI, 18-19). These are the words spoken by Jesus to Peter when he, alone among the Apostles, replied to his Saviour's question – 'Who am I?' – in these words: 'You are Christ, the Son of the living God' (*Matthew*, XVI, 16). At this the Messiah changed Simon's name and transformed his life, calling him 'Peter', the stone on which rests the whole earthly structure of Christian spirituality: the Church of God. The episode that literally changed the destiny of the world is open to numerous interpretations, beginning with the one that compares a man to the architecture of a building, and makes him the 'cornerstone' of the whole Christian spiritual structure. It is no coincidence that Jesus, as told in the *Gospel of John* (II, 19), stated that he would 'rebuild' the Temple in three days, alluding to his own body in this architectural metaphor. In similar manner, in two passages from the *First Epistle to the Corinthians* (VI, 15, w19), traditionally attributed to St. Paul, Jesus asks his brothers in Christ, very simply and clearly: 'Do you not know that your bodies are members of Christ?', and again, 'Do you not know that your body is the temple of the Holy Spirit that is in you?'

Façade of St. Peter's Basilica.

St. Peter's Square

In the light of all this, calling Peter the 'cornerstone' of the spiritual, as well as material, edifice planned by Christ assumes a value that is even greater, if possible. Martyred on the Vatican Hill during the reign of Nero (54-68) and buried there, Peter and his 'Trophy' are the 'pillar of faith', exactly coinciding with the present-day altar in the great Basilica. During the persecutions of Emperor Valerian (253-260) the cult of the Apostle was probably moved somewhere near St. Sebastian's cenotaph, while his relics remained on the hill, as indicated by the fact that this was the site where Constantine (306-337) had a Basilica built starting in 324, which was consecrated in 326 and completed in 349. It was an immense structure with five

Exterior of the Dome over St. Peter's Basilica.

naves and a T-shaped transept, which became a model for later churches. Before the Basilica was an arcaded courtyard, known as the Paradise Court. At its centre stood the famous *Pigna* (the gigantic 'pinecone' now in the Cortile della Pigna of the Vatican Museums), which pilgrims used to touch as soon as they arrived here. Various documents give some idea of the appearance of the old St. Peter's, beginning with the drawings of Giacomo Grimaldi (Biblioteca Apostolica Vaticana, cod. Bar. 2733) depicting the Basilica before it was partially demolished and rebuilt in the 16th century. St. Peter's was an obligatory stage in the pilgrimage to Santiago de Compostela (for travellers coming from the south) and a necessary stopping point on the road to Jerusalem (for those coming from the north), as well

Interior of the Dome over St. Peter's Basilica.

as a holy site that drew throngs of Christians from all over Europe. When the first Jubilee was held in 1300, the Constantinian Basilica was already nearly a thousand years old. Giotto celebrated this event with the famous mosaic (now lost) of the *Navicella*, the ship of the Church steered by the Prince of Apostles. Despite constant maintenance and improvements starting with the loggia built under Pope Boniface VIII Caetani (1294-1303), Christianity's most important church had arrived at the point of collapse. Although it was Pope Nicholas V Parentucelli who made the decision to rebuild St. Peter's, systematic work on this project began only in 1506 under Julius II Della Rovere. On April 18, 1506, the Della Rovere pope descended into the foundations of the Constantinian Basilica accompanied by a group of cardinals and laid the first stone at the base of what was to become the *Pier of the Veronica*.
The first among the Apostles, on whom Jesus had vowed to build his Church, would thus have the largest and most majestic church in the Christian world. On the rich marble flooring, in fact, are indications of the interior lengths of some great temples of Christianity, ranging from St. Paul's in London (the largest) to St. Patrick's

in New York (the smallest), that could all fit into St. Peter's Basilica, which has a length of 186.36 meters and a maximum width of 137.85 meters at the transept.
This was the idea of Julius II: a grandiose temple at the centre of which would stand his tomb, already commissioned from Michelangelo. With the death of the pope, this ambitious project was of course abandoned and the heirs of Julius II had to content themselves with a tomb in the church of San Pietro in Vincoli (St. Peter in Chains), also in Rome, which contains Michelangelo's *Moses* (1513), one of the statues planned for the original project. The new Basilica was designed in the shape of the *crux gammata* of Jerusalem, elaborated by Donato Bramante (1444-1514).
The idea, as has been demonstrated by art historians, was that of presenting St. Peter's as the Heavenly Jerusalem, since the Greek cross plan allowed for four chapels at the corners, of the same shape as the first but smaller. As a whole, this was an expression in masonry of the emblem of the Holy City par excellence, with four crosses lying within the arms of the great cross.
At the death of Bramante, a commission of architects was set up, directed by Raphael (1483-1520), with Giuliano da Sangallo (1443/45-1516) and Fra Giocondo da Verona (1433-1515) as the other members. In the new project Bramante's solution was abandoned in favour of a Latin cross plan with a colonnaded pronaos. Raphael died in 1520 and was succeeded by Antonio da Sangallo the Younger (1484-1546) and Baldassarre Peruzzi (1481-1536), who changed the project again, planning a building midway between those proposed by the other two architects.
It was, in fact, a church shaped like a Greek cross, whose western arm was lengthened by another chapel. Remaining from this project is the gigantic wooden model, big enough to stand up in, commissioned in 1538 by Paul III Farnese (1534-1549) from Sangallo, who took eight years to build it.
The plan was finalized at last, still under Pope Paul III, who appointed Michelangelo Buonarroti Architect of the Fabric of St. Peter's. The appointment was made on January 1st, 1546 and the assignment was to last until the great artist's death. With Michelangelo (1475-1564) came a partially definitive solution: a return to Bramante's design, but simplifying it and conferring on it great majesty. The plan was that of the Greek cross, and the central dome now assumed a predominating role.
At Michelangelo's death he was succeeded by Vignola (1507-1573), Pirro Ligorio (1510/13-1583), Giacomo Della Porta (1532/33-1602) and Domenico Fontana (1543-1607), who erected the obelisk at the centre of the plaza that was to become St. Peter's Square. Later, Pope Paul V Borghese (1605-1621) objected that the church, as it had been designed, would be too small to welcome all of the pilgrims flocking to it. The task of enlarging it was assigned to Carlo Maderno (1556-1629), who added an extension to Michelangelo's design, changing the plan of the Basilica to that of a Latin Cross. For centuries, this architect from Ticino was accused by all of having 'ruined' the project of the genius par excellence, a paltry accusation considering that Maderno's work opened the way to the Baroque style, which was then splendidly expressed by Gian Lorenzo Bernini (1598-1680) in the interior decoration. For the broad façade completed in 1612 – in the seventh year of the pontificate of Pope Paul V Borghese, as states the inscription on the architrave – Maderno chose the giant order, derived from the architecture of Andrea Palladio (1508-1580). Classic and majestic, the 'giant order' consists of Corinthian columns and pilasters ex-

Vico Consorti, *Holy Door (Porta Sancta)*, 1949, St. Peter's Basilica.

Gian Lorenzo Bernini, *Baldachin*, 1624-1633, St. Peter's Basilica.

tending along the double register of the doors and windows. At the centre is the *Loggia of the Blessings*, at the sides the two *Clocks* added by Giuseppe Valadier (1762-1839). On the balustrade stands a row of statues as high as 7.50 meters, with the Saviour, St. John the Baptist and other saints at the centre.
The atrium at the entrance is 71 meters long and 13 meters wide. Finished at the same time as the façade, it was decorated starting in 1618 with stuccowork representing scenes from the New Testament and episodes from the *Life of Christ*. Five bronze doors open into the Basilica. At the centre is the oldest of them, the *Filarete Door* (*Porta Filarete*), named for the artist who carved it for Pope Eugene IV Condulmer (1431-1447). The *Holy Door* (*Porta Sancta*), the last on the right, which is opened and closed again by the pope every 25 years at the beginning and end of a Holy Year, or Jubilee, was carved in 1949 by Vico Consorti and inaugurated for the Jubilee of 1950. The *Door of Death* (*Porta della Morte*) was completed by Giacomo Manzù in 1964. The *Door of the Sacraments (Porta dei Sacramenti*) was made by Venanzo Crocetti (1960) and the *Door of Good and Evil (Porta del Bene e del Male*) was carved for Pope Paul VI Montini (1963-1978) by Luciano Minguzzi (1977).
Upon entering the Basilica, visitors are struck by the harmonious ensemble and the grandiose interior, whose enormous size is not immediately apparent. It becomes clear, however, in approaching the *Font* designed by Agostino Cornacchini (1686-1754), to find that the charming little angels adorning it are over 2 meters high. Here everything is colossal, but so well-proportioned that this is hard to realize. In facing the inner façade, for example, looking away from the apse, the pilaster strips are 23 meters high. The inscription on the architrave the last verse of the above-mentioned passage from Matthew (XVI, 18-19), where Jesus tells Peter that whatever he binds on earth will also be bound in heaven, like everything he will loose ('SOLUTUM ET IN COELIS') – is 1.40 meters high, and is written on a gilt band 3 meters wide. Note, then, the *Clocks*, designed by Giuseppe Valadier, like those on the façade. The one on the left tells time according to the 'French' system (showing the 12 hours), the other according to the 'Italian' system, as was customary in the Papal State up to 1846, with only 6 hours.

Gian Lorenzo Bernini, *Throne of St. Peter*, 1657-1666, details, St. Peter's Basilica.

Continuing to walk along the main nave, before reaching the *Font*, we find among the intarsia on the floor the *Rota porfiretica*, or coronation wheel, a great disk of red porphyry, the only remaining element from the central nave of the old Constantinian St. Peter's. On it kneeled the twenty-three sovereigns crowned by the popes between 800 and 1452, from Charlemagne to Frederick III.

The opulent interior decoration was created over the centuries, with supreme skill and consistency. Michelangelo had planned a bare interior, marked only by its architectural elements, like the *Medici Tombs* in Florence. Pope Gregory XIII Boncompagni revised the great artist's plans starting from the Gregorian Chapel. Begun by Michelangelo in 1561 and continued by Vignola, it was completed by Giacomo Della Porta with coloured marble and inlaid semi-precious stones between 1567 and 1573. In 1598 the mosaic decoration of the dome was begun, to cartoons painted by the Cavalier d'Arpino (1568-1640). However, the interior of the Basilica as it appears today is mainly the work of Gian Lorenzo Bernini. He not only decorated the pillars in the naves and the gigantic piers supporting the dome – planning the great statues of *Saint Veronica* by Francesco Mochi (1640), *Saint Helena* by Andrea Bolgi (1640), *Saint Andrew* by François Duquesnoy (1640) and *Saint Longinus* (1638), his own work – but also invented the bronze 'theatrical machines' of the *Baldachin* and the *Throne of St. Peter*, or *Cathedra Petri*.

Art historians deem them strikingly theatrical effects, and in this connection it should be recalled that Bernini, a theatre-lover and playwright, was accustomed to creating stage sets and temporary decorations for the great festivals that marked the life of the city. Accordingly, in place of the classic ciborium, he imagined an immense processional *Baldachin* that seems placed there at the end of one of the many religious processions parading through the Rome of the popes. To build the *Baldachin*, he used bronze taken from the roof of the Pantheon, provoking Pasquino's famously sarcastic comment, '*Quod non fecerunt Barbari, fecerunt Barberini*' ('What the barbarians did not do, the Barberini did'). It was, in fact, Pope Urban VIII Barberini who authorized this despoiling of the Pantheon, viewed by the Romans as an insult to one of the city's finest monuments.

The results, however, were extraordinary: the *Baldachin* (completed in 1633) is one of the masterpieces of Baroque sculpture and architecture. The four twisted columns, evocative of the Temple of Solomon, rest on four marble blocks, designed and carved by Francesco Borromini (1599-1667). They bear the coats of arms of the Barberini family, appearing in an allegory representing the Church giving birth to Truth. Borromini represents every stage of childbirth through the changing expressions of the figure. In shape, the columns reflect the stone ones of the *pergula* (altar screen decoration) in the old St. Peter's (now set into the sides of the four niches in the piers supporting the dome), thought to come from the Temple of Solomon. The columns of the *Baldachin*, however, are populated by cupids, various animals such as bees (symbol of the Barberini family) and even lizards, appearing among the gilt-bronze laurel leaves. The bees also allude to the concept of Truth and light, since they produce wax, the material of holy candles, as had been written in the *Exultet*. Another decorative element is the sun, a visual metaphor of God, Christ and Truth. Above, four enormous Cherubim watch over the throne of God. The *Baldachin* is in fact a baroque transposition of the ancient Arc of the Alliance (which, with the Tables of the Law given to Moses, symbolized the pact between God and the People of Israel) and is placed over the *tomb of St. Peter*, designated 'foundation of the Church' by Christ the Saviour, which incar-

Arnolfo di Cambio, *St. Peter, c.* 1290, detail, St. Peter's Basilica.

nates the new Alliance, the new pact with God stipulated through the Redemption. The culminating point of the Basilica's symbolic and architectural structure is, however, the *Throne of St. Peter*, or *Cathedra Petri*. This great structure made of bronze, gilt bronze, stuccowork and glass encloses a chair whose acacia wood structure may date from the time of the Prince of Apostles, but not the ivory decorations, which are from the Carolingian age, like the portrait of the sovereign resembling Charles the Bald.

Antonio del Pollaiolo, *Monument to Innocent VIII*, 1484-1492, detail, St. Peter's Basilica.

The throne has not been displayed in public since 1867, and the faithful must be content with a copy in the Basilica's Museum of the Treasury. The *Cathedra* on which Peter is said to have sat is, in fact, enclosed in the immense bronze chair 7 meters high, supported by four bronze statues representing the Doctors of the Church: Augustine and Ambrosius for the Western Church, Athanasius and John Crisostomos for the Eastern Church. Above, Angels in Glory appear among the golden clouds and at the centre, daylight from the window is transmuted into mystic light as it falls through glass painted with an image of the Dove of the Holy Spirit. This great 'theatrical machine', created by Bernini and his assistants between 1657 and 1666, is a worthy conclusion to the itinerary of faith and art through the Basilica, which, however, holds still more treasures. Unforgettable among them is the bronze statue of *St. Peter*, attributed to Arnolfo di Cambio (c. 1245-1302), but which may instead be a work from Late Antiquity, whose foot has been worn smooth by the kisses of the faithful; and the Chapel of the Pietà with Michelangelo's *Pietà*, the only statue signed by the great master, sculpted in 1499.

The last act of this exceedingly long history is the colonnade, built at the initiative of Pope Alexander VII Chigi (1655-1667) to provide temporary shelter for the faithful waiting to be blessed.

Bernini designed it – recalls his son Domenico, his first biographer – as an embrace endowed with a triple value; for catholics, to confirm them in their faith; for heretics, to reunite them to the Church; and for infidels, to enlighten them with the true faith. It is the embrace of Peter that leads to Christ. From here, looking upward, the great dome can be seen, rising over 136 meters above the ground,

Antonio Canova, *Tomb of the Stuarts*, 1817-1819, St. Peter's Basilica.

with an outside diameter of nearly 60 meters. Designed and built by Michelangelo up to the drum, it was then continued by Giacomo Della Porta and Domenico Fontana up to the lantern (on whose top the cross was placed in 1593).
St. Peter's, the place where two Ecumenical Councils have been held (Vatican I in 1869-1870 and Vatican II in 1962-1965), is also the seat of major religious events such as canonizations and beatifications. It has always been considered the very symbol of Catholic Christianity.

Antonio del Pollaiolo, *Monument to Innocent VIII*, 1484-1492, St. Peter's Basilica.

List of popes mentioned

Index of Names

Index of Names

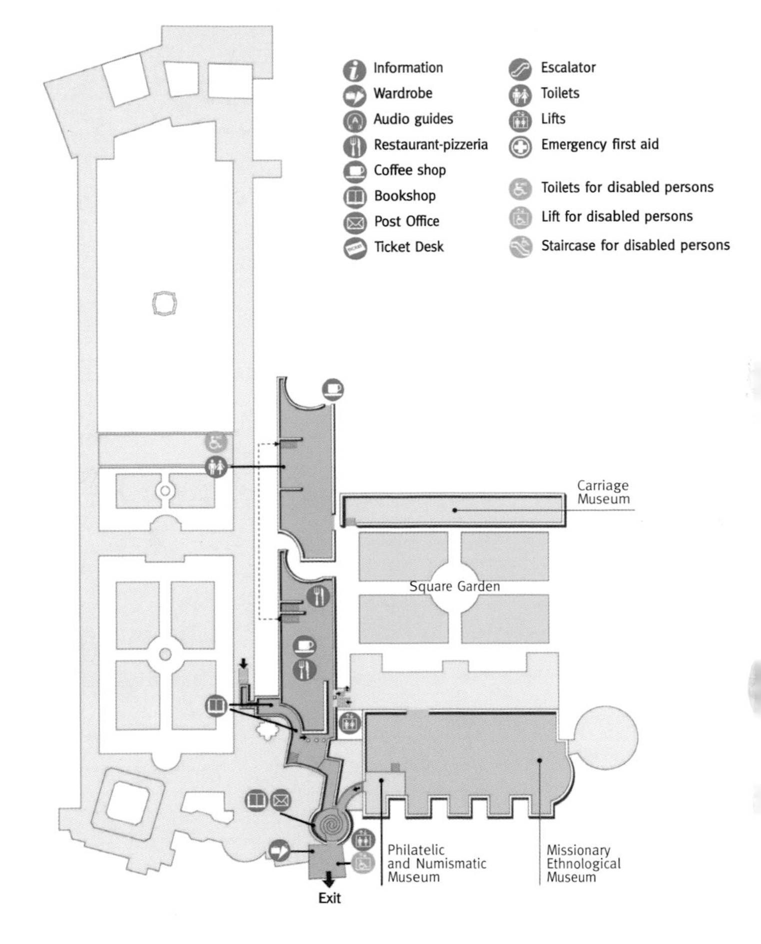
Information
Wardrobe
Audio guides
Restaurant-pizzeria
Coffee shop
Bookshop
Post Office
Ticket Desk
Escalator
Toilets
Lifts
Emergency first aid
Toilets for disabled persons
Lift for disabled persons
Staircase for disabled persons
Carriage Museum
Square Garden
Philatelic and Numismatic Museum
Missionary Ethnological Museum
Exit